Cit

Independence Educational Publishers

First published by Independence Educational Publishers

The Studio, High Green

Great Shelford

Cambridge CB22 5EG

England

© Independence 2013

Photocopy licence

The material in this book is protected by copyright. However, the
purchaser is free to make multiple copies of particular articles for instructional
purposes for immediate use within the purchasing institution.
Making copies of the entire book is not permitted.

British Library Cataloguing in Publication Data

Citizenship in the UK. -- (Issues ; v. 240)

1. Citizenship. 2. Civics, British. 3. Political participation--Great Britain.

I. Series II. Acred, Cara.

323.6'0941-dc23

ISBN-13: 9781 86168 638 1

Printed in Great Britain

MWL Print Group Ltd

Contents

Introduction

Citizenship in the UK is Volume 240 in the **ISSUES** series. The aim of the series is to offer current, diverse information about important issues in our world, from a UK perspective.

ABOUT CITIZENSHIP IN THE UK

Citizenship education explores ideas of identity, belonging and responsibility. Today, many ethnic minorities living in the UK identify more strongly with the concept of "Britishness" than their white counterparts. But what does being British actually mean? This book explores the importance of citizenship education, the concept of identity in the UK, the role of the Government and how to become an active citizen. It also highlights and breaks down the roles of the monarchy and Parliament in the UK.

OUR SOURCES

Titles in the **ISSUES** series are designed to function as educational resource books, providing a balanced overview of a specific subject.

The information in our books is comprised of facts, articles and opinions from many different sources, including:

- Newspaper reports and opinion pieces
- Website fact sheets
- Magazine and journal articles
- Statistics and surveys
- Government reports
- Literature from special interest groups

A NOTE ON CRITICAL EVALUATION

Because the information reprinted here is from a number of different sources, readers should bear in mind the origin of the text and whether the source is likely to have a particular bias when presenting information (or when conducting their research). It is hoped that, as you read about the many aspects of the issues explored in this book, you will critically evaluate the information presented.

It is important that you decide whether you are being presented with facts or opinions. Does the writer give a biased or unbiased report? If an opinion is being expressed, do you agree with the writer? Is there potential bias to the 'facts' or statistics behind an article?

ASSIGNMENTS

In the back of this book, you will find a selection of assignments designed to help you engage with the articles you have been reading and to explore your own opinions. Some tasks will take longer than others and there is a mixture of design, writing and research based activities that you can complete alone or in a group.

FURTHER RESEARCH

At the end of each article we have listed its source and a website that you can visit if you would like to conduct your own research. Please remember to critically evaluate any sources that you consult and consider whether the information you are viewing is accurate and unbiased.

What is citizenship education?

We want young people to leave school or college with an understanding of the political, legal and economic functions of adult society, and with the social and moral awareness to thrive in it.

Citizenship education is about enabling people to make their own decisions and to take responsibility for their own lives and their communities.

It is not about trying to fit everyone into the same mould, or about creating 'model' or 'good' citizens.

We want our schools and colleges not simply to teach citizenship but to demonstrate it through the way they operate.

Why teach citizenship?

Democracies need active, informed and responsible citizens; citizens who are willing and able to take responsibility for themselves and their communities and contribute to the political process.

Democracies depend upon citizens who, among other things, are:

⇨ aware of their rights and responsibilities as citizens;

⇨ informed about the social and political world;

⇨ concerned about the welfare of others;

⇨ articulate in their opinions and arguments;

⇨ capable of having an influence on the world;

⇨ active in their communities;

⇨ responsible in how they act as citizens.

These capacities do not develop unaided. They have to be learnt. While a certain amount of citizenship may be picked up through ordinary experience in the home or at work, it can never in itself be sufficient to equip citizens for the sort of active role required of them in today's complex and diverse society.

If citizens are to become genuinely involved in public life and affairs, a more explicit approach to citizenship education is required. This approach should be:

⇨ inclusive: an entitlement for all young people regardless of their ability or background;

⇨ pervasive: not limited to schools but an integral part of all education for young people;

⇨ lifelong: continuing throughout life.

And, as Democratic Life points out, citizenship is the only subject in the national curriculum that teaches about the way democracy, politics, the economy and the law work.

Citizenship issues are:

⇨ real: actually affect people's lives;

⇨ topical: current today;

⇨ sometimes sensitive: can affect people at a personal

level, especially when family or friends are involved;

⇨ often controversial: people disagree and hold strong opinions about them;

⇨ ultimately moral: relate to what people think is right or wrong, good or bad, important or unimportant in society.

How does it benefit young people?

It helps them to develop self-confidence and successfully deal with significant life changes and challenges such as bullying and discrimination;

It gives them a voice: in the life of their schools, in their communities and in society at large;

It enables them to make a positive contribution by developing the expertise and experience needed to claim their rights and understand their responsibilities and preparing them for the challenges and opportunities of adult and working life.

Who else does it benefit?

Citizenship also brings benefits for schools, other educational organisations and for society at large.

For schools and other educational organisations, it helps to produce motivated and responsible learners, who relate positively to each other, to staff and to the surrounding community. For society it helps to create an active and responsible citizenry, willing to participate in the life of the nation and the wider world and play its part in the democratic process.

What are its essential elements?

Citizenship education involves a wide range of different elements of learning, including:

⇨ Knowledge and understanding: about topics such as: laws and rules, the democratic process, the media, human rights, diversity, money and the economy, sustainable development and world as a global community; and about concepts such as democracy, justice, equality, freedom, authority and the rule of law;

⇨ Skills and aptitudes: critical thinking, analysing information, expressing opinions, taking part in discussions and debates, negotiating, conflict resolution and participating in community action;

⇨ Values and dispositions: respect for justice, democracy and the rule of law, openness, tolerance, courage to defend a point of view and a willingness to: listen to, work with and stand up for others.

The most effective form of learning in citizenship education is:

⇨ active: emphasises learning by doing;

⇨ interactive: uses discussion and debate;

⇨ relevant: focuses on real-life issues facing young people and society;

⇨ critical: encourages young people to think for themselves;

⇨ collaborative: employs group work and co-operative learning;

⇨ participative: gives young people a say in their own learning.

This text is based on Chapter One of the CPD handbook *Making Sense of Citizenship*.

2010

⇨ The above information is reprinted with kind permission from the Citizenship Foundation. Please visit www. citizenshipfoundation.org.uk for further information.

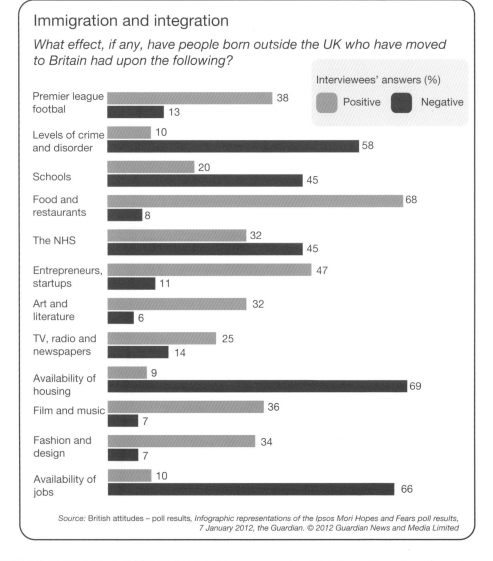

Immigration and integration

What effect, if any, have people born outside the UK who have moved to Britain had upon the following?

Interviewees' answers (%)
Positive   Negative

	Positive	Negative
Premier league footbal	38	13
Levels of crime and disorder	10	58
Schools	20	45
Food and restaurants	68	8
The NHS	32	45
Entrepreneurs, startups	47	11
Art and literature	32	6
TV, radio and newspapers	25	14
Availability of housing	9	69
Film and music	36	7
Fashion and design	34	7
Availability of jobs	10	66

Source: British attitudes – poll results, *Infographic representations of the Ipsos Mori Hopes and Fears poll results, 7 January 2012, the Guardian.* © 2012 Guardian News and Media Limited

© *Citizenship Foundation 2012*

United Kingdom: facts

Information from the European Union.

Year of EU entry: 1973

Political system:
Constitutional monarchy

Capital city: London

Total area: 244 820 km

Population: 61.7 million

Currency: pound sterling

The United Kingdom (UK) consists of England, Wales, Scotland (who together make up Great Britain) and Northern Ireland. The UK's geography is varied, and includes cliffs along some coastlines, highlands and lowlands and many islands off the coast of Scotland. The highest mountain is Ben Nevis in Scotland which reaches a height of 1,344m.

The United Kingdom is a constitutional monarchy and parliamentary democracy. The main chamber of parliament is the lower house, the House of Commons, which has 646 members elected by universal suffrage. About 700 people are eligible to sit in the upper house, the House of Lords, including life peers, hereditary peers, and bishops. There is a Scottish parliament in Edinburgh with wide-ranging local powers, and a Welsh Assembly in Cardiff which has more limited authority for Welsh affairs but can legislate in some areas.

The English account for more than 80% of the population. The Scots make up nearly 10% and the Welsh and Northern Irish most of the rest. The UK is also home to diverse immigrant communities, mainly from its former colonies in the West Indies, India, Pakistan, Bangladesh and Africa.

The economy – one of the largest in the EU – is increasingly services-based although it maintains industrial capacity in high-tech and other sectors. The City of London is a world centre for financial services.

Home of the Industrial Revolution, the United Kingdom has produced many great scientists and engineers including Isaac Newton and Charles Darwin. The father of modern economics, Adam Smith, was a Scot. English literature has produced an endless stream of poets, dramatists, essayists and novelists from Geoffrey Chaucer via Shakespeare and his contemporaries to a plethora of modern writers such as J. K. Rowling and the Nobel Prizewinner, Doris Lessing.

There are many regional and traditional specialities to tempt the visitor to the United Kingdom. For example, in Scotland you might try Arbroath smokies (lightly cooked smoked haddock), or in Northern Ireland why not start your day with an Ulster fry (fried bacon, egg, sausage, soda farls and potato bread)? A traditional speciality in Wales is laverbread (seaweed) made into small cakes with Welsh oatmeal, fried and served with eggs, bacon and cockles. A traditional dish from the north of England is the Lancashire hotpot made with lamb or beef, potatoes and onions.

2012

⇨ The above information is reprinted with kind permission from the European Union. Please visit www.europa.eu for further information.

What does the Union Jack mean to you?

Monarchy, empire, Olympics...racism? Pan-GB poll compares Scotland, Wales and England views.

By Bonnie Gardiner and Hannah Thompson in Editor's picks and Life

People in England, Scotland and Wales most associate the Union Jack (often called simply the 'Union Flag') with monarchy, the British Empire and sacrifice in the World Wars, a recent poll on British attitudes to nationality, for think tank British Future, has found.

Key findings

⇨ The Union Jack is most commonly associated with the Monarchy, the British Empire and the British Armed Forces across England, Wales and Scotland

⇨ The flag is also associated with pride, patriotism, democracy and tolerance

⇨ Scottish people are less likely than English or Welsh to associate the Union Jack with patriotism

⇨ Scottish respondents are more likely to associate the Union Jack with racism and extremism

⇨ English public are more likely to associate the flag with upcoming Olympics and 'Team GB'.

Flying the flag for...

⇨ Strong majorities of respondents from all three nations polled associated the monarchy with the Union Flag. 84% of English respondents, 82% of Welsh and 80% of Scottish

⇨ Around three in five to two thirds associate the Flag with the British Empire (English 64%, Welsh 60% and Scots 60%)

⇨ While 'sacrifice in the World Wars' was also a popular association, with 68% of the English, 63% of the Welsh and just over half of Scots (55%)

⇨ The British Armed Forces were associated with the Union Jack by the majority of each country's respondents (English 80%, Welsh 77% and Scots 70%).

Patriotism...and racism

The Union Jack is also associated with ideals of pride and patriotism, democracy and tolerance, our poll found, but although a good percentage of Scots are similarly inclined, more Scots than English or Welsh associate the flag with negative connotations such as racism and extremism.

⇨ 80% of English respondents associated the Union Jack with pride and patriotism, along with 68% of Welsh respondents and just over half of Scots (56%)

⇨ Around two in five (41%) of Scottish respondents associate the Union Jack with democracy and tolerance compared to over half of the English (54%) and just under half of the Welsh (47%)

⇨ And while 15% of English respondents and 16% of Welsh associated the Union Jack with racism and extremism, a full 25% of Scots said that they associated the flag with this.

Modern and diverse Britain?

The flag on balance receives less backing when it comes to associating it with a modern and diverse Britain, and when used in a 'modern sense', looks to be received best by the English public rather than Britain as a whole – for example, more English people that Welsh or Scottish associate the flag with the upcoming Olympics and 'Team GB', or pop music.

⇨ 37% of English consider that the Union Jack represents a modern and diverse Britain, compared to 30% of Welsh and 25% of Scots

⇨ 75% of English people associate the flag with 'Team GB' and the London 2012 Olympics, compared to 63% of Welsh people and just over half of Scots (55%)

⇨ Around a third of English respondents (34%) thought the Union Jack could be associated with British pop music, compared to 24% of Scots and just 13% of Welsh respondents.

Historically, the origin of the term 'Union Jack' – a national flag that incorporates the symbols of three countries: England (with Wales), Scotland and Northern Ireland – is uncertain, but harks back to a time in which it was most commonly used by the armed and naval forces.

There are various theories as to whether the flag should be referred to as 'Jack' or merely 'Union Flag' with the 'Jack' ostensibly only correct when not on dry land but nowadays it seems that the terms are used interchangeably.

Independent identities

Many Britons believe that, as the national flag incorporates the symbols of all UK countries, the 'Union Jack' emphasises the very nature of the United Kingdom: perpetuating diversity, unity and strength.

However, the issue of independence and devolution remains pertinent, especially regarding recent calls from Scottish Minister Alex Salmond to vote on the issue of independence north of the border.

Anti-independence commentators, however, claim that should Scotland be granted independence, it could damage their identity as Britons, and the unity of the nation itself. Vicky Wong writes on online news site PolicyMic, 'independence [seems] very romantic … but not only could it lead to the break-up of an ancient union, it could make both Scotland and the new UK weaker players on the international stage'.

Hitting back at claims that independence could threaten Britain's economic power and dilute the British identity, however, Scottish National party MSP for Glasgow, Humza Yousaf, has said that any country that makes up the union would not lose its identity or diminish the importance of Britain by becoming independent of it, but rather would celebrate their national identity and role in the British community, as well as 'welcoming a broad and diverse future'.

'Independence is the broad, inclusive and positive option for Scotland, in which the wide range of identities we have in our modern nation – Scottish, British, Pakistani, Chinese, Polish, Irish and many, many more – can all be reflected and celebrated,' he said.

1 May 2012

⇨ The above information is reprinted with kind permission from YouGov. Please visit www.yougov.co.uk for further information.

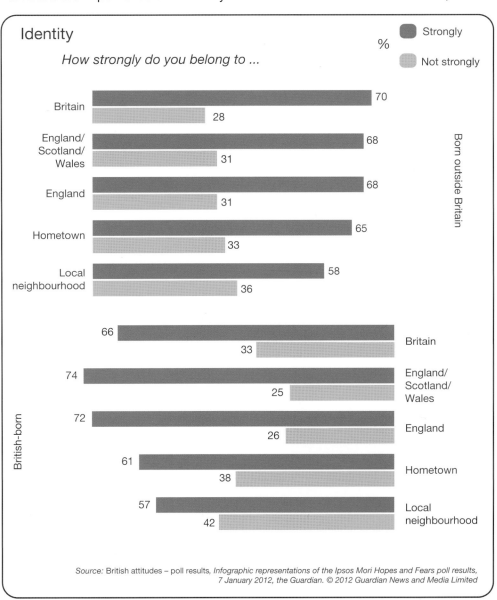

Identity

How strongly do you belong to ... %

Strongly

Not strongly

Born outside Britain

	Strongly	Not strongly
Britain	70	28
England/Scotland/Wales	68	31
England	68	31
Hometown	65	33
Local neighbourhood	58	36

British-born

	Strongly	Not strongly	
66	33		Britain
74	25		England/Scotland/Wales
72	26		England
61	38		Hometown
57	42		Local neighbourhood

Source: British attitudes – poll results, *Infographic representations of the Ipsos Mori Hopes and Fears poll results, 7 January 2012, the Guardian. © 2012 Guardian News and Media Limited*

(Dis)united kingdom?

Information from British Future, a non-partisan think tank.

People across Britain want Scotland to stay in the United Kingdom

Scotland will hold a referendum on whether to be independent before 2015. But what difference would it make if that were held across the UK? The British Future State of the Nation poll found that there are currently strikingly similar views opposing Scottish independence across Scotland, England and Wales (with the main difference being a lower proportion of don't knows in Scotland) and there are broadly similar views across Britain about English devolution too.

Flying all the flags: why we don't want to choose between our identities

The poll suggests that there is no sharp clash between English and British identities – indeed quite the opposite.

A sense of belonging to Britain and local pride goes together for most people – or tends to be weaker across the board – in England especially, while Scottish and Welsh identities are held strongly by those who feel British as well as by those who don't.

In England, those who feel that they belong to Britain and to their local areas have a strong sense of English identity too. 92% of those who feel they strongly belong to Britain also say that they strongly belong to England, with only 8% of the strongly British saying they did not belong strongly to England too. But a strong sense of English identity fell to 27% among those who did not have a strong sense of being British, with 60% saying they did not feel strongly English. 83% of those who feel they have a strong sense of belonging to their neighbourhood had a strong sense of being English, falling to 44% among those without a strong sense of local belonging.

Geordies feel less British than the Scots

Our poll found a weaker commitment to British identity in the north-east of England than in Wales or Scotland. Only 49% of people in the north-east feel strongly British, much lower than the 67% who feel strongly British across England as a whole. While 62% of Welsh people and 60% of Scots feel strongly British, with 37% and 40% disagreeing.

Asians feel strongly British

Asians in Britain have the strongest sense of British belonging, with 70% saying they belong strongly, compared to 66% of white Britons.

English identity is slightly stronger among the white people in England, where 72% feel strongly English and 27% don't, but is not much lower among ethnic minorities in England, where 62% feel strongly English (including 69% of Asians) and 34% don't. Perhaps showing that Englishness is now considered a civic rather than an ethnically defined identity.

January 2012

⇨ The above information is reprinted with kind permission from British Future, a non-partisan think tank. Please visit www.britishfuture.org for further information.

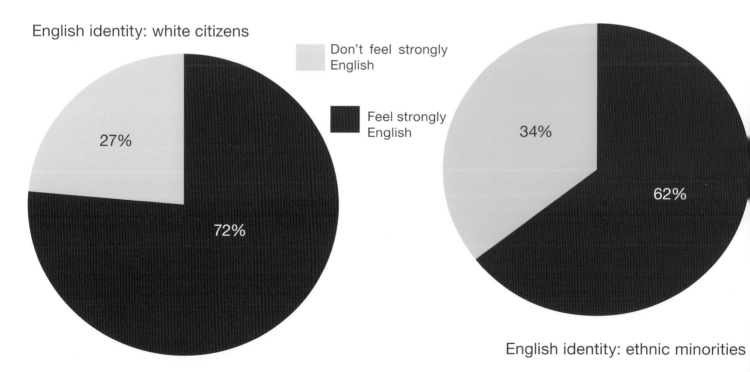

English identity: white citizens

Don't feel strongly English

Feel strongly English

27%

72%

34%

62%

English identity: ethnic minorities

Citizenship test to be rewritten by the Government

The test taken by foreign nationals who wish to become British citizens is to be rewritten by the Government, according to reports.

By Tom Lawrence

Immigrants will have to learn the first verse of the national anthem and be tested on key historical facts as part of the overhaul designed to place a greater focus on the nation's culture and past, *The Sunday Times* said.

A new handbook, expected to be issued in the autumn, will be issued to prospective citizens and form the basis of the modified 45-minute exam all aspiring British citizens must pass.

It will tell immigrants the UK is 'historically' a Christian country with a 'long and illustrious history' and include sections about key battles as well as British inventions, discoveries and culture.

A section on the Queen will also be included, with would-be-Britons also expected to memorise the profiles of famous artists, writers and playwrights such as William Shakespeare.

The Life in the United Kingdom test was originally introduced by Labour in 2005.

But Home Secretary Theresa May believes it places too much emphasis on the practicalities of daily living in Britain rather than the country's history, according to the newspaper.

She is understood to have scrapped sections dealing with claiming welfare payments, borrowing money and the Human Rights Act.

A Home Office spokesperson said: 'Putting our culture and history at the heart of the citizenship test will help ensure those permanently settling can understand British life, allowing them to properly integrate into our society.'

1 July 2012

⇨ The above information is reprinted with kind permission from *The Independent*. Please visit www.independent.co.uk for further information.

Regional nationalism

Devolution in Scotland and Wales has led to self-governing nations within the UK. In both countries there are high levels of pride at the national or regional level but there are stark differences in how pride in Scotland and pride in Wales impact on patriotism in Britain as a whole.

Overall, in looking at England, Scotland and Wales, it is clear that English people have a weak conception of 'English nationalism' while Scottish people have a strong sense of 'Scottish nationalism' and a weaker sense of 'British nationalism'. Meanwhile Welsh people have been able to combine a strong sense of 'Welsh nationalism' with a strong sense of 'pride in being British'.

More than three-quarters – 81 per cent – of English people agreed with the statement 'I am proud to be a British citizen'; the number of Welsh people who were proud to be British citizens was only slightly lower at 75 per cent, but the number of Scottish people who were proud to be British citizens was substantially lower at 61 per cent. Surprisingly, the Welsh were the most likely to agree with the statement 'I am proud of Britain's role in the world'. Over 50 per cent of English people agree with this statement, over 55 per cent of Welsh and 46 per cent of Scots.

Our survey also asked respondents to complete the sentence 'I am proud to be from...' and given the options 'my city/town/village, my country or region, my part of the UK (e.g. England, Scotland, Wales), Great Britain, Europe, the World as a whole, another country, or other'. Almost three in ten respondents in England and Wales stated 'Great Britain', compared with just 15 per cent of Scottish respondents. Scottish people are less likely to state that they are proud to be a British citizen than the Welsh and English.

It is clear that regional and national patriotism does not necessarily correspond with a breakdown in support for, and pride in, Great Britain and the UK. Welsh citizens felt most comfortable and confident articulating their support for Britain in the world and their pride in our national actions while maintaining significant pride in their home nation. In this sense, as with ethnic and religious identities, regional and national identities within the UK need not be seen as threats to patriotism in Britain – indeed, they may even be helpful in bolstering and supporting pride. It is possible that Welsh identity – having been sufficiently expressed through the National Assembly and cultural institutions – helps to support the higher levels of pride in Britain's role in the world in Wales.

However, Scottish citizens are less adept at combining their Scottish identity with their British identity – choosing on the whole to take pride in one or the other. This presents a very real threat to British patriotism as Scottish identity appears to be displacing a wider sense of British pride rather than reinforcing or coexisting with it. It is possible that the political use of patriotism by the Scottish National Party has contributed to this phenomenon.

February 2011

⇨ Information from Demos. Please visit www.demos.co.uk.

© Demos 2011

Key polling results

Regional nationalism

⇨ When asked to complete the sentence 'I am proud to be from...' and given the option of 'my city/town/village, my country or region, my part of the UK, (e.g. England, Scotland, Wales), Great Britain, Europe, the World as whole, another country, or other', almost 3 in 10 English and Welsh respondents stated 'Great Britain' but only just over 15% Scottish respondents stated 'Great Britain'.

⇨ 62% of Scots cited 'my part of UK (e.g. Scotland, Wales or England) compared with 50% of Welsh and 24% of English respondents.

⇨ 17% of English respondents said 'my city/town/village' compared with 6% of Welsh and 8% of Scots respondents.

⇨ 13% of English respondents said 'my region or county' compared with 8% of Welsh and 3% of Scots respondents.

⇨ Of the regions, respondents from London were the most likely to cite 'Great Britain'.

⇨ 28% of respondents in urban areas cited 'Great Britain', compared with 27% in 'town and fringe' and 20% in rural areas.

⇨ Almost 36% of English respondents strongly agreed with the statement 'I am proud to be a British citizen', compared with 29% of Welsh and 21% of Scots respondents.

⇨ Respondents in the North-East and North-West of England were most likely to 'strongly agree' with the statement.

Hurt pride

⇨ 54% of respondents agreed with the statement 'Sometimes I am embarrassed to be British'.

⇨ 61% of Scots respondents agreed with the statement compared with 53% of English and 46% of Welsh respondents.

Have the Olympics ushered in a new, positive Britain?

Britain is having a post-Olympic bounce; feeling a bit more confident, a bit more enthusiastic, and a bit more sporty than we did before.

Given the whirlwind of winners, anthems, and evenings when it didn't seem possible to watch anything but the Olympics whatever the sport, Britain is feeling a bit more able to say to the world that 'look this is who we are' and we are feeling pretty good about it, and we are feeling it might change Britain for ever.

Critics might have lapsed back into a post-Olympic slump, but they have not taken the public with them. Buoyed by the feeling of connection during the Games, we are now feeling surprisingly positive that it will have a long-term impact, and confident in a Britain that reflects who we are today.

Not surprisingly there has been a shift in how many people think that the Olympics could be good for British mood, with a high 80% saying it has been, compared with 53% who thought it would be a good mood boost when British Future polled the question in December last year.

The reality has exceeded expectations, and how often can we say that? The combination of superb medal-winning achievements, an Olympic park that worked, avoiding a transport meltdown and a genuinely impressive opening ceremony has given the British public an uplift. When it comes to considering if the Olympics is making a difference to how the rest of the world perceives Britain, our expectations before the event were lower than now, after the Olympics has finished. That figure has bounced from a net positive of 56% (with 23% being very positive) before Christmas, to a much bigger 73% thinking Britain has impressed the globe with its innovation and sporting achievement, and of that overall figure, those thinking the Olympics will have a very positive effect on the way Britain is viewed by the rest of the world has bounced to 41%. All in all, we are feeling confident that

Britain has shined up its global image, having proved that we can innovate and impress, while delivering massive projects on time. After all, who knew?

That doesn't mean that Brits are walking around in a rose-tinted haze though, they are still realistic about the challenges ahead. Back in December, 52% were optimistic about 2012 for them and their family, and 26% pessimistic, and as the Olympics ended 47% were saying the year had been good so far, and 27% bad for them and their families. The majority felt it had not been a great year for Britain or Europe.

But despite the economic hard times, there was a massive vote for big events such as the Jubilee and the Olympics not being a waste of time and cash, with only 22% thinking they were an unnecessary distraction, and 70% saying that 'events like this bring people together and improve the mood of the nation' and 58% agreeing that the Olympics will leave a long-lasting positive impact on British society. That's a big yah boo sucks to those people who moaned about it all being a giant waste of money which could be better spent on something else. Actually it turns out to be a once in a lifetime experience for most of us, and unforgettable. Right now it also feels like a spectacular win for Britain, something that made a difference to our lives like nothing else could.

And going forward will it change anything? Will we find a new Britain or a Britain with a new attitude?

Our polling suggests there is a genuine belief that it could be, with 79% of the public believing it will increase our sporting participation, and 50% believing there will be an increase in volunteering on the back of our pride in the enthusiastic Games Makers, who made such a difference to our attitude to life.

So to keep this new Britain feeling more positive, and more confident, what do we need to do? Well, there's a feeling that Brits could start by spending less time knocking ourselves, and more time taking pride in our achievements, with 65% agreeing that Brits don't talk about the good things often enough. We are the nation that loves to knock success, and takes pride in cutting those with giant egos down to size. It would be a shame to lose that infamous British sarcasm, but could we combine it with a bit more positivity? If so, comedians and news programmes might suffer. Around 64% of Brits felt the British media doesn't do us any favours by generally lashing on the misery in its coverage of life and the universe, although that certainly wasn't true during those two recent heady weeks. We seemed to have recognised a different kind of Britain, one that we are happier with, one that represents who we actually are. While 66% agreed (12% disagreed) with the reviewers that Danny Boyle's Olympics opening ceremony reflected the best of traditional and modern Britain, a sizeable 75% agreed that the Olympics showed that Britain was a confident, multi-ethnic society. For most of us it is that memory of a confident, happy Britain that will stick with us, and our surprised pleasure at being part of a crowd, in a street, in a shop or around a television who just wanted to cheer on the team, and feel part of something great in Britain.

20 August 2012

⇨ The above information is reprinted with kind permission from British Future, a non-partisan think tank. Please visit www.britishfuture.org for further information.

© *British Future 2012*

Team GB: 'Plastic Brits' – where do they come from?

The British Olympic team contains 60 'plastic Brits' – Britons born aborad – in its 542 members. But where were they born?

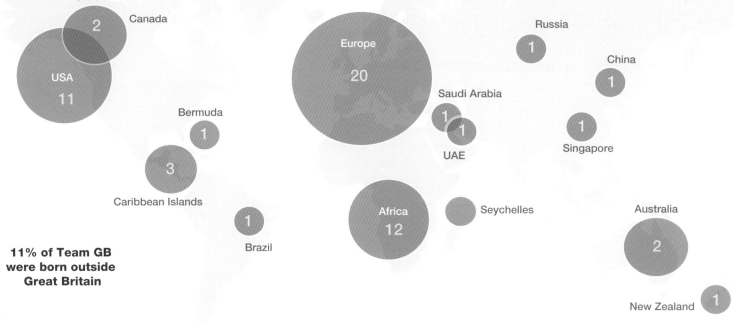

11% of Team GB were born outside Great Britain

Let's peel the 'plastic' label off Team GB's foreign-born athletes

***Information from** The Huffington Post.*

By Josh Cowls

As Stephen Hull was right in pointing out earlier this week, the media has been expending plenty of column inches and airtime lamenting various aspects of the upcoming Olympic Games. Make no mistake: the failure of G4S to provide the requisite security staff is a true debacle, and lampooning a pitiful British summer has always been fair game. But one of the less helpful stories to have emerged in recent weeks is the discussion of so-called 'Plastic Brits': members of the British Olympic team who were born overseas.

The Telegraph has compiled a rather elaborate infographic to illustrate the point. It shows that 60 of Team GB's 542 athletes were born overseas, which, at first glance, seems like quite a lot. Nation states are the basic currency of the Games, with national anthems, flags and kits providing so much of the iconography at each Olympiad, so the idea that national borders are so permeable to sports people might seem to pose a threat to this core principle.

But delve a little deeper into *The Telegraph*'s list, and the whole concept of 'Plastic Brits' basically melts away. First of all, some of Team GB's leading lights, like Bradley Wiggins and Beth Tweddle, make the list by virtue of being born abroad to British parents. Who knew Wimbledon regular Laura Robson was born abroad? More to the point, who cares?

This raises a problem for proponents of the 'Plastic Brits' idea. As soon as one or two technically foreign-born athletes are deemed 'British enough' to take part (and find me anyone who would deprive cycling supremo Wiggins of a shot in the Olympic time trial), plausibly anyone else born outside the country also has a claim to compete under the British flag. This is where the argument gets messy – how do you define 'sufficient Britishness'?

Residence in the UK? Having two British parents?

The obvious but important answer is that we don't decide who does and who doesn't qualify as British – that's the job of the Home Office and Border Agency. As such, each of the 60 foreign-born Team GB athletes is a British citizen with a British passport, and they couldn't compete otherwise. Thus, changing immigration law would be the only way to affect the Olympic selection policy on the grounds of nationality.

In any case, pointing out that particular legal nicety isn't the primary aim of this article. My main point is that by looking at these 'Plastic Brits' as the real people and exceptional athletes that they are, rather than through the crude, futile lens of 'sufficient nationalism', the stories you find show our country at its open, plural and dynamic best.

Take the story of Luol Deng, the NBA basketball star so valuable that UK

Basketball is paying some £300,000 just to insure him against injury. Born in what recently became independent South Sudan, Deng and his family fled unrest and were granted political asylum in the UK. Deng's formative years spent in Brixton undoubtedly helped him reach the heights of the NBA. Or look at Mo Farah, who could win two medals on the track in London. Born in Somalia, Farah moved to Britain where it was a PE teacher who spotted and nurtured his talent for long-distance running, in spite of Farah's initially limited English.

Then there is the sub-category of athletes who have competed under different flags in past competitions. If anything, the biographies of some of these competitors are even more remarkable. Yamile Aldama, the triple jumper who will turn 40 a fortnight after competing in London, has actually represented two countries already, her native Cuba and Sudan. Having married a Scottish husband she emigrated here in 2001 and applied straight away for a British passport. Only after a decade, which she lived through in incredibly tough circumstances as a single mother in virtual poverty, was Aldama awarded what she craved: British citizenship and with it the right to compete under the Union Jack.

Finally, consider the case of long jumper Shara Proctor, who was born and competed for Anguilla before switching to the British team in 2010. The thing is, Anguilla is not an independent country but a British Overseas Dependency, meaning it doesn't actually have the ability to send athletes to the Games under its flag. One wonders whether some of the same people offended by recent Argentinian propaganda showing a hockey player training on the Falklands are those who decry 'foreign' competitors like Proctor competing for Team GB.

Of course, by 2016 Britain's sports authorities may be dealing with an entirely new set of problems over nationality. With the looming referendum over Scottish independence in 2014, in four years' time we may be speculating over the eligibility of such sporting stars as Sir Chris Hoy and Andy Murray to compete under the British flag. I somehow doubt that a 'Plastic Scots' debate would be any more enlightening or helpful than the present 'Plastic Brits' question.

Ultimately, each of the 542 athletes who compete for Team GB in London has earned their right to be there. So this summer let's cast aside the 'Plastic' label and let each athlete have their moment in the sun. Metaphorically, at least.

21 July 2012

⇨ Article written by Josh Cowls for *The Huffington Post* and is reprinted with permission. Please visit www.huffingtonpost.co.uk.

Half of UK voters want 'British values' prioritised

More than half of British voters would be willing to back a party that promised to "prioritise traditional British values over other cultures", a survey of the levels of support for UK extremist groups has revealed.

By Jennifer Lipman

Fifty five per cent of those questioned in a poll conducted by YouGov for the Extremis Project, a group tracking the rise in far-right politics, said a party running on this platform would be more likely to win their support.

More than a third of the cross-section of 1,725 people said parties espousing an anti-Islamic stance or pledging to reduce the number of Muslims and the presence of Islam in society would be likely to get their vote.

Two out of five of those questioned said they would support politicians who promised to curb all immigration.

Despite the views expressed, more than half of all respondents indicated that an increase in levels of support for extremism would worry them.

'While underlying cultural tensions still concern large numbers of citizens, we also found that younger generations are far more relaxed about diversity and immigration,' said Dr Matthew Goodwin and Anthony Painter, founders of the Extremis Project.

'This provides more evidence that there are sharp generational differences in our attitudes toward these issues, and that mainstream parties that "talk tough" on these issues risk alienating an emerging, and more tolerant generation of voters.'

'The results show that immigration and culture are issues that can cause serious tension in certain conditions,' said Dave Rich of the Community Security Trust, adding that these were 'precisely the issues that extremist parties try to exploit'.

'The survey shows there is still work to be done in reducing intolerance and guarding against extremist parties.'

20 September 2012

⇨ Information from *The Jewish Chronicle Online*. Please visit www.thejc.com.

Identity crisis: are we becoming a disunited kingdom?

Surveys suggest notions of Britishness are changing. The Guardian *invites readers to share their views on national identity.*

By Severin Carrell

So what makes us? We share the same islands, but we aren't all British. We call ourselves Scots, Irish, Welsh, English and often, but decreasingly, British. Every four years, we rally to the union flag for the Olympics, but when it comes to rugby and football, the divisions open up.

There is much shared culture, whether on pop music, clothing, fish and chips, curries and Marmite, comedians and *Coronation Street*. We also cringed at Tony Blair's attempt to exploit the notion of 'Cool Britannia' in the euphoria of his 1997 election victory.

But now, for the first time in several centuries, that notion of Britishness is under intense strain. Alex Salmond, the First Minister of Scotland, will soon lead the country into a referendum that could prompt Scotland to declare independence, a move that would shatter a 304-year-old political union.

Regardless of the Scottish referendum, the UK has four separate governments and now the three devolved administrations, in Scotland, Wales and Northern Ireland, are winning greater economic and legal powers, cutting London's grip on the country. And in each part of the UK, notions of nationhood and Britishness are changing and, arguably, the links are weakening.

Because of this unfolding political situation, *The Guardian* invites readers to enter the debate about national identity and air your attitudes on Britishness. An interactive graphic will allow us to map the evolving identities across the UK in advance of a series of special reports on the country. We will be asking if it is more and more becoming a 'disunited kingdom'?

There is much to suggest this is the case. John Curtice, from the Scottish Centre for Social Research, is co-author of the *Scottish Social Attitudes* survey. He said: 'The crucial thing to realise is that in Scotland, British is now very definitely a secondary identity; that's undoubtedly true to a far greater extent than it is in Wales.' In England there are plenty of people who, if asked whether they're British or English, will say 'what's the difference?'.

Comparing all the latest social attitudes surveys gives us this contrast: if voters are forced to choose, 52% of English voters choose British first compared to 19% of Scots, and 30% of Welsh.

Intriguingly, the latest evidence from Wales suggests that devolution may be making the Welsh feel more British. That is one reading of a new study of 3,029 voters by the Economic and Social Research Council, carried out in the run-up to the 2011 referendum, which found overwhelming support for giving the Welsh Assembly greater powers.

Its results, published here for the first time, find that 16% of Welsh voters now feel 'British not Welsh', compared to 9% in 2007 and in 2003. Meanwhile, only 19% felt 'Welsh not British', a fall from 24% in 2007, with 30% feeling equally Welsh and British.

Roger Scully, from Aberystwyth University and the study's co-author, is cautious about reading too much into the Welsh figures since different survey methods were used in 2011.

'The bigger picture is that basic identity in Wales has not changed much under devolution, or even if you go back and look at the evidence from 1979, since the first devolution referendums,' he said.

'People have very different views now about how Wales should be governed. But not because they have become, in some crude sense, more Welsh.'

In Northern Ireland, identity can be far more complex; loyalty to a larger nation splits between those feeling British and Irish, mostly down religious or ethnic lines. The 2010 Northern Ireland Life and Times surveys, the equivalent of the British Social Attitudes survey, have shown that 37% see themselves as British, 26% Irish and 29% Northern Irish, with 3% choosing Ulster.

But asked the multiple-choice question, 58% of voters in Northern Ireland in 2007 saw themselves, to varying degrees, as both British and Irish. In 1998, 51% of those given a straight choice said they were British. It is 37% now.

In England last year, 52% described themselves as British and just 34% as English in a straight choice between the two. That is the widest margin since 1997.

Behind such figures emotions run deep. Yet, is national identity in the UK purely a personal badge to be worn with pride at sporting events – or could it fundamentally change the nature of British (and Northern Irish) state. You tell us...

6 October 2011

⇨ The above article originally appeared in *The Guardian* and is reprinted with permission. Please visit www.guardian.co.uk for further information.

What does Britishness mean to you?

We asked people across Britain for their ideas on national identity.

Nadia Hussain, 32, biomedical scientist, Stratford, East London

My parents came here from Pakistan in 1974. I was born in Forest Gate, East London, in 1979. I experienced a lot of racism growing up. The racial groups – white, black, Asian – tended to keep in their own groups. It was really weird. But I love the East End, and wouldn't change it for the world. Our neighbours are white, and we love them to bits. Britain is moving too fast and has lost its sense of Britishness. It's obsessed by money, and social bonds are breaking down. I'm proud to be British, but the country isn't as strong as it was. Our educational system is deteriorating, unemployment is rising, and I worry about the future. The Olympics will be great, but what happens afterwards?

Alicia Jones, 16, student, Caernarfon, Gwynedd

It's language not politics that mainly identifies us here. I can write English, but find it a bit difficult to speak it. I would like there to be a separate Wales so that we could be our own country. At least then we would be more in control. It would just be about Wales, and we could generate our own jobs. I don't know if we could do it, but we should give it a go.

Tom Stinchcombe, 23, student, Hasting, East Sussex

I'm originally from Bristol, but am now studying at the University of Brighton. I consider myself British rather than English. Scotland, England and Wales need to stick together. Britishness means living under a democracy and having the freedom to do what you want with your life. The Queen may not embody Britishness (I don't relate much to the Queen and her jubilee), but Parliament does. It's a unique institution. The economic situation worries me and capitalism as we know it isn't working to everybody's benefit, but there is still much to admire in this country. We are more questioning and more secular than the US, and have true freedom of speech. It's important for my generation not to buy into the Britain-in-decline idea.

Sagir Ahmed, 41, careers adviser, Bradford, West Yorkshire

My parents are from Kashmir, and I see myself as a British Kashmiri. My dad had an uncle who drove trolley-buses in Bradford, and he joined him here in 1962 to work in the mills. I am a Kashmiri nationalist, and belong to the Jammu Kashmir Liberation Front (JKLF) since I was 18. I've only been to Kashmir once, but the heritage is very important to me. I'm proud of being British, but my roots are in Kashmir. Culturally, my ideas are partly British and partly Kashmiri. I like to think I balance the two.

David Sinclair-Benstead, 67, retired hospital chef, Stratford, East London

I was born in Scotland, but have lived most of my life in England. I have never lost my Scottishness, but feel British and wouldn't support Scottish independence. It's possible to be four separate countries, but also to come together as Britain. For me, Britishness means the royal family and tradition. The jubilee is a big moment. It's important because of what the Queen has given to the country, but also what she stands for – stopping dictatorship. She is only a figurehead, but she still, theoretically, has the power to veto any Acts of Parliament. Britishness also means quirky things such as morris dancing and cheese rolling. Stupid things like that are essentially British, and I hope we never lose them.

Amanda Thompson, 32, income recovery officer, Belfast, Northern Ireland

I don't see myself as British or Irish. I'm from a mixed marriage. My mum is a Protestant and sees herself as British; my dad is Catholic and sees himself as Irish; I see myself as Northern Irish because this is where I'm from. I was brought up Catholic, but when I was younger I was never actually taught the difference. My mum and dad didn't like the Troubles and the problems here, and they brought me up never to identify with all the sectarianism.

5 February 2012

⇨ The above article originally appeared in *The Guardian* and is reprinted with permission. Please visit www.guardian.co.uk for further information.

How to be British

Information from HelloGiggles.

By Liza Baron

For my first HelloGiggles column, I wanted to introduce myself by way of a quick guide to being British. I am British through and through – I love queuing, I like being kept on my toes by the changes of seasons and I love that I live on this tiny little island that speaks so loudly to the world. I am a bit obsessed with current affairs and always have my nose stuck into what's going on, whether it's from following Twitter trends, watching reality TV or reading the broadsheets. The UK creates so much beautiful art, music and style – I hope HG readers from the UK, US and all round the world like hearing what I have to say about it all. Here's my little guide on how to be British.

Obsessively read fashion tips in magazines, blogs, columns and tweets…then go right on ahead and ignore them: Look, our seasons change every five minutes and we just can't scrape together enough pennies to keep updating our wardrobes all the time. Better to choose a funky signature style and stick to it (perhaps with a few catwalk-inspired adjustments or accessories). I think of my style as casual-pretty meets old-lady-vintage; a style based around a good selection of dresses that I can dress up with heels and lippy or down with trainers and a nice warm cardigan. Yes, I said cardigan.

Watch soaps: The whole of Great Britain is split between those who watch *Eastenders* (me!) and those who watch Coronation Street, but the main thing is to pick a side and stick to it. Through thick and thin, on holidays and dull working weeks alike, you can always rely on the fact that the people on the soaps are having a harder time than you are. Apparently some people claim not to watch soaps. These people are lying.

Complain when your favourite show is remade for a US network: …but secretly prefer the NBC version. *The Office*, anyone?

Make the most of summer festivals: I've been to Glastonbury festival almost every year since I was born, and love that many other boutique-y festivals have sprung up all over the country. Nothing says being British more than watching your favourite band in the rain whilst wearing a pretty summer dress and wellies.

Get really, REALLY excited when your country's sports teams make it to international events …and then pretend the whole thing never happened when they get knocked out in the second round. *cough*every worldcupsince1966*cough*. I don't even like football much, but I can't help but get swept up in the hype.

Speaking of hype, get hyped. About anything and everything: For a small country, we have a lot going on – get involved. Don't pretend you're not excited about the 2012 Olympics – we all are – so let's just admit it and enjoy the togetherness of it all.

Be slightly uncomfortable when you talk about the Royal Family: Kate's done wonders for their public image, but is it OK to be fond of the Royals? Nobody knows!

Get on yer bike! There's nothing like going on a bike ride with a good friend, getting covered in mud, and letting her giggle at you for the rest of the trip. I'm more often a cycle-to-work kinda girl – you get to be smug about doing regular exercise but chances of getting muddy are minimal.

Slag off your country when it suits – but ultimately be patriotic: You know how you can slag off your sister to anyone who'll listen, but woe betide anyone else who says anything negative about her? That.

Exaggerate your accent to sound cute: Whenever I speak to someone from the US, Australia or another English-speaking country, I find myself getting more and more British-sounding by the second. I even said 'cheerio' on the phone the other day. I'm going to visit New York in March and have already started practising my best Queen's English! And boys, we know you do it too.

Drink tea. Lots of it: 'Nuff said.

23 January 2012

⇨ The above information is reprinted from HelloGiggles. Please visit www.hellogiggles.com.

How diverse is the UK?

Information from the Institute for Social & Economic Research.

By Alita Nandi and Lucinda Platt

Immigration into the UK is a hotly debated and electorally salient topic. In popular and political discourse immigrants are perceived as a threat not only to labour market or housing prospects of those settled for longer, but also to cultural continuity. Immigrants are frequently represented in popular politics and media as being additional or extraneous to the population rather than core to its make-up. This contrasts with some other countries where immigration is regarded as part of the national story even if immigration controls are nonetheless relatively stringent.

The UK has also been characterised throughout its history as a country of multiple populations: more distantly Celts, Romans, Anglo-Saxons, Jutes, Norse, Normans, French, Dutch and those fleeing religious persecution in Europe; more recently, those from other European countries, those who arrived through the extensive trading networks of the British Isles, and those with colonial links with the UK. The largest immigrant flows in recent years have been from the A8 countries, from Anglophone countries such as US, New Zealand and Australia and from the pre-2004 EU countries. Running throughout the history of the UK are substantial population flows to and from (the Republic of) Ireland.

Moreover, the UK itself is a multiple nation, made up of four countries with populations who identify themselves, and are recognised, as distinct.

This article therefore sets out to consider two questions. First: how diverse is the UK in terms of ancestry and heredity, self-perception and identification with being British? Second: is self-categorisation as ethnic majority or as minority ethnic linked to feelings of 'Britishness'?

Here we can exploit the fact that Understanding Society has questions on own, parental and grandparental country of birth, on own and parents' ethnic group, as well as questions on Britishness.

Questions on parental and grandparental country of birth were asked of 47,710 adults (16+ years) living in the sampled households who participated in the interviews conducted between 2009 and 2010. The question on Britishness was asked of a smaller group of 17,680 adults. Weights were used to adjust results for sample design and non-response.

Within the UK population, 72% was born in England, 9% in Scotland, 5% in Wales and 3% in Northern Ireland. We find that 11% of the UK population was born outside the UK, but 29% of the UK population has some connection with a country outside the UK (that is, either own, parents' or grandparents' birth country is outside UK). Thus the composition of the UK looks substantially more diverse if we take into account the parentage of the UK population going back just two generations. On the other hand, claims to the UK being a diverse nation should not be overemphasised: 48% of the UK population are only associated with England. That is, nearly half of

the UK population does not even have connections to the smaller countries of the UK in the last two generations and have family links only within England.

Looking together at ethnic identification and countries respondents are associated with suggests that there is substantial level of 'assimilation' to majority (White British) identification over even a relatively small number of generations. This is found among a proportion of those born outside the UK, as well as among those with connections to other countries but born within the UK. While 29% are associated with a country outside the UK, only 14% of the UK population define themselves as of minority ethnicity (3.6% of which are White Other). In fact, 52% of those who have some connection outside the UK define themselves as White British, while 17% of those who were not born in the UK call themselves White British. Among those with parents from different ethnic groups, 30% call themselves 'mixed' but 35% of them call themselves White British. How should we view this? On the one hand this might be regarded as a positive 'melting pot' story. On the other, there might be regret at the relative absence of 'hyphenated' or multiple identities which allow the maintenance of cultural claims.

Second, more people are associated with a country outside the UK than were born there or define their ethnicity in terms of it. For example, among UK residents 3.4% were associated with India, while 1% were born in India and 2% chose the category 'Indian' as their ethnic group. Again, 7% have parents or grandparents from the Republic of Ireland while 1% define themselves as Irish, though even fewer, 0.7%, were born there.

Finally, we explored what, if any, was the relationship of the expressed ethnic identity and claims to Britishness. It might be a reasonable expectation that those who maintain – or are ascribed – a minority ethnicity might feel less connected to notions of Britishness.

We next investigated whether ethnic category and subjective assessments of identity intersect. We found that, after adjusting for sex, age and education (because younger and more highly educated people express a lower sense of Britishness), those of minority ethnicity typically express a stronger British identity than the White British majority. This is true of UK and non-UK born minorities (though the non-UK born across all groups express a lower sense of British identity). It is not, though, true of those affiliating to a 'mixed' identity. Unsurprisingly, we found that those living in Scotland and Northern Ireland had lower

British identification (on average) than those living in England and Wales.

On the other hand, for those describing themselves as White British, being born outside the UK has a negative effect on British identity. That is, those who 'assimilate' to White Britishness, have a lower sense of British identity than those who maintain a minority identity. Both these patterns are opposite to what might be assumed if the expectation was that expressed identity was meaningful for national connections.

In conclusion, there are far more people in the UK with non-British origins than those who say their ethnic group is not White British. In other words, many of the people whose parents or grandparents were born outside the UK define themselves as White British. Thus the apparently homogenous majority is more diverse than is typically represented. On the other hand, there is a substantial English core of the UK population: half of the UK population were born in England as were their parents and grandparents.

Finally, it is clear that expression of minority identity does not imply alienation from national identity ('Britishness'), and nor does majority ethnic affiliation bring with it a stronger endorsement of national identity.

February 2012

⇨ The above information is reprinted with kind permission from the Institute for Social & Economic Research. Please visit www.understandingsociety.org.uk for further information.

© 2012 Institute for Social & Economic Research

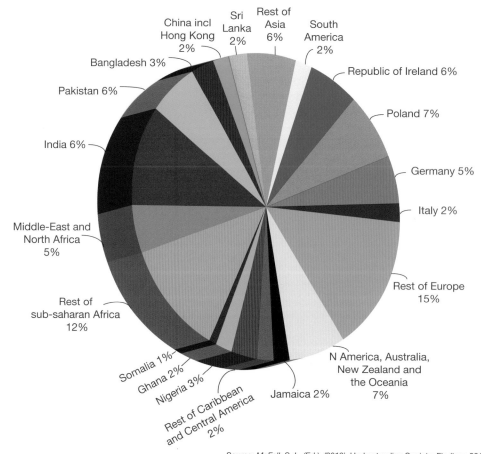

Distribution of UK population by country of birth for those born outside of the UK

Source: McFall, S. L. (Ed.). (2012). Understanding Society: Findings 2012. Colchester: Institute for Social and Economic Research, University of Essex. © 2012 Institute for Social & Economic Research

Muslims are well-integrated in Britain – but no one seems to believe it

British Muslims often express a stronger sense of belonging than other citizens, so why are they still seen as outsiders?

By Leon Moosavi

In Britain today there is a mismatch between how non-Muslims often perceive Muslims and how Muslims typically perceive themselves. This disconnect is down to a tendency by non-Muslims to assume that Muslims struggle with their British identity and divided loyalties. These concerns were challenged a few days ago, in a report by the University of Essex that found Muslims actually identify with Britishness more than any other Britons.

This study is just one of several recent studies that have consistently found that Muslims in Britain express a stronger sense of belonging in Britain than their compatriots. Consider the following examples:

⇨ 83% of Muslims are proud to be a British citizen, compared to 79% of the general public.

⇨ 77% of Muslims strongly identify with Britain while only 50% of the wider population do.

⇨ 86.4% of Muslims feel they belong in Britain, slightly more than the 85.9% of Christians.

⇨ 82% of Muslims want to live in diverse and mixed neighbourhoods compared to 63% of non-Muslim Britons.

⇨ 90% of Pakistanis feel a strong sense of belonging in Britain compared to 84% of white people.

Those who work closely with Muslim communities will attest to the integrated position of British Muslims and that despite frequent exoticisation, British Muslim lives are much the same as any other citizen's. British Muslims also appreciate their ability to practise their religion in Britain without the type of subjugation that fellow Muslims are subjected to under despotic regimes in several Muslim-majority countries. Even though negative depictions may encourage people to imagine Muslims as similar to the 7/7 bombers who struck seven years ago this week, your average British Muslim is much more likely to be similar to a confident Amir Khan, a bubbly Konnie Huq or a hard-working James Caan.

There is, quite frankly, no major issue of Muslims not wanting to be a part of British society. But there is an issue with the common but unspoken xenophobia pervasive in British society that casts Muslims as outsiders. That is why despite Muslims repeatedly pledging their dedication to Britain, a consistent spattering of polls show that many non-Muslim Britons still view Muslims as a potential enemy within. Consider the following examples:

⇨ 47% of Britons see Muslims as a threat.

⇨ Only 28% of Britons believe Muslims want to integrate into British society.

⇨ 52% of Britons believe that Muslims create problems.

⇨ 45% of Britons admit that they think there are too many Muslims in Britain.

⇨ 55% of Britons would be concerned if a mosque was built in their area.

⇨ 58% of Britons associate Islam with extremism.

The minority of Muslims in Britain who do view Britain with contempt – as indeed, we must recognise there are some – frequently explain their disaffection as a result of being labelled as outsiders and told they do not belong. Thus, the inability to appreciate British Muslims as typical citizens can actually create the very atypical citizens that are feared in the first place. Muslims want to be part of British society but their marginalisation may lead to some retreating to the margins.

If the myth that Muslims in Britain will not integrate is allowed to be propagated, it will only lead to the continuation of a harmful cycle whereby greater distrust and animosity is sown. The results of this can be devastating. Last Sunday marked the three-year anniversary of the Islamophobic murder of Marwa El-Sherbini by a far-right attacker, a crude example of an inability to accept that Muslims are at home in Europe. This intense rejection of Muslims is increasing across Europe, which is especially disturbing considering that a significant number of the far right would consider armed conflict against Muslims, as the case of Anders Breivik revealed. In Britain, we have seen several far-right plots that seek to undermine the presence of Muslims in British society, such as a recent arson attack on a mosque in Stoke-on-Trent. Clearly, there are weighty consequences to the dismissal of Muslims as fellow British citizens.

While politicians may claim that multiculturalism has failed, there is a strong case to be made that it operates successfully every day when Britons of different faiths, ethnicities and backgrounds convivially co-operate alongside each other to make the nation what it is today. Muslims are integrated, feel at home in Britain and are quite simply as British as the next person, even though this does not quite match the sensationalised cynicism that some enjoy indulging in. This rather unexciting conclusion is actually rather exciting as it lays to bed many of the unwarranted concerns that are held about British Muslims.

3 July 2012

⇨ The above article originally appeared in *The Guardian* and is reprinted with permission. Please visit www.guardian.co.uk.

Why do non-white Brits feel that little bit more British?

Information from British Future, a non-partisan think tank.

By Sunder Katwala

Ethnic minorities living in Britain identify more strongly with 'Britishness' than do their white counterparts, *The Times* reports this weekend (£, paywall), as it previews a huge 40,000 strong *Understanding Society* survey from the Institute for Social and Economic Research and the Institute for Education.

The newspaper notes that the results 'fly in the face of suggestions that ethnic groups are unable or unwilling to integrate'.

Asked 'how important is being British to you?' the average scores by ethnicity on a 0-10 scale were as follows:

Pakistani (7.76), Bangladeshi (7.75), Indian (7.68), Black African (7.64), Middle Eastern (7.48), Other (7.03), Chinese (6.90), Caribbean (6.89), Mixed race (6.78), White (6.58).

The research also finds that people in Wales have a slightly stronger sense of Britishness than the English, while there is a weaker British identity in Scotland – with an average score of 6.30, compared to 7.44 in Wales.

Surveys consistently find that a majority of Scots (around six in ten) do have a strong sense of British identity, though less intense than their Scottish identity for most, but about three in ten reject being British entirely, saying they are Scottish, not British.

In England, the Midlands (7.38) and London (7.34), perhaps a little boosted by minority patriotism, have a stronger sense of British identity than the north (7.24) or the south outside London (7.11). The research will be presented by Dr Alita Nandi at the ESRC research methods festival in Oxford next week.

The reported findings are consistent with several other surveys, including an Ipsos MORI poll carried out for British Future, which have consistently found strong British patriotism among ethnic minorities is often just that little bit stronger than among the general population.

'Ethnic minorities living in Britain identify more strongly with "Britishness" than do their white counterparts'

As I wrote in *The Observer* in January, of the *State of the Nation Hopes and Fears* report published (PDF file) for the launch of British Future: 'Our poll also finds that ethnic minorities feel just a little more proud to be British than white Brits, and immigrants most optimistic about the future. That could be good news for integration, as long as we pay more attention to those who fear being left behind". The Demos *A Place For Pride* report the previous Autumn also generated headlines such as Muslims "are more patriotic than most British people' in the *Daily Mail*.

This raises two intriguing questions.

Why would those from minority backgrounds feel not only just as patriotic as the majority of people, but more so? And why is this consistent finding so often greeted as a surprising revelation?

The Times columnist David Aaronovitch today writes that 'it shouldn't really be a shock', noting a parallel with the history of immigration and integration of British Jews across the last century.

'My immigrant grandparents were illiterate and my grandmother was one of those recalcitrant women, much maligned these days, who never mastered English. Perhaps part of her always remained gossiping over the washing in some village on the shifting Polish-Russian frontier. Their children, however, were not Russian or Polish. They were British. Today you will walk many a country mile before you encounter anybody more British than the Chief Rabbi Lord Sacks. The very expectation on the part of others that it would be otherwise – this Britishness of the newcomer – may itself help to intensify it.'

However, the desire of minorities to integrate is not, in itself, enough to create a sense of belonging. The desire to be integral to society has to be reciprocated too, in terms of the opportunity to belong to the national community, as well as in terms of socio-economic inclusion. So the long-term intergenerational decline in racism in British society is also an important and necessary condition for integration and patriotism.

It is very difficult to go around shouting 'There ain't no black in the Union Jack' as the National Front used to in the 1970s, and also say 'why don't these people want to be like us?'.

We naturally, and correctly, think that racism is wrong because it is unfair to the individual or group denied fair treatment and equal opportunity because of prejudice.

'Why would those from minority backgrounds feel not only just as patriotic as the majority of people, but more so?'

Less often discussed is another social cost of racism: that racism also presents an important barrier to the integration into a shared society that most white citizens, as well as most from ethnic backgrounds, say that they want.

Another question is how much integration a liberal society believes that it needs for a shared society. There is a strong pro-integration preference among minorities – for civic and political participation, democracy and the rule of law, and most recognise the importance of the English language for social, economic and civic inclusion. What is difficult is if those demands go further into a demand for complete assimilation, demanding a severing of all cultural connections and affinities, or creating a culture which discourages freedom of religious expression, as for example in some continental European countries discouraging the building of mosques or minarets. These 'pro-integration' demands risk crossing the boundary to where they will repel the thing that they claim to want. Yet Britons could agree on this too: most people agree that the Tebbit test takes a step too far.

But I am not sure we should fully understand this phenomenon as being solely about the keenness of newcomers to fit in. The claim to British identity can be about a deep sense of shared history too, particularly for those non-white Britons from Commonwealth countries. The issue is not just claiming a voice in helping to shape a common future. It is also about reminding ourselves that, complicated and contested though it certainly was, we have shared

more history than we think. You can look for and find British Muslim patriotism in reports from the First World War trenches, and not only in the last few years.

If every silver lining has a cloud, perhaps we should ask too why white Britons have, on average, a slightly weaker sense of British identity. This should not be overstated: the differences are not particularly wide, and the lower Scottish sense of British belonging is distinctive. (The challenge there is to ensure the Scottish identity is civic and inclusive, for those who reject British identity.)

Previous survey evidence tends to support what we might observe anecdotally: that there are different reasons for a weaker sense of national identity among some white Britons.

One group who find flag-waving unnecessary or unattractive are super-cosmopolitan liberals, especially in London, who can be found on both the socially liberal left and centre, and on the pro-market liberal right. This reflects both a commitment to individualism over collectivism and, perhaps especially, an under-examined confidence about identity, which leads to a failure to understand why it does matter to others, as David Skelton noted in a recent blog for *The Huffington Post*.

'Of more pressing concern is a weaker sense of identity among those who feel socially, economically and politically excluded'

A relative lack of feeling for national identity among this group helps to explain why British identity matters less to graduates than non-graduates. Graduates, on average, score 6.87 on the Britishness scale, behind those with no formal qualifications (7.68), O-levels or GCSEs (7.43) and A-level or equivalent (7.18). The implication of the different scales reported is that white, left-leaning graduates will

tend to score lower than those who are either from a minority group or who are Conservative supporters.

The non-patriotism of this secure, educated and mostly affluent group is, for the most part, probably mostly pretty harmless, though it was amusingly anatomised in George Orwell's *The Lion and the Unicorn* in 1940, in a period when its consequences might have been more serious. Its over-representation among opinion formers can lead to a rather skewed instinct for what most people think and feel, from both right and left of centre voices. A secure internationalist cosmopolitanism is usually founded on being able to take the protections of a nation state and a passport for granted, which is why the keenness of British refugees to participate in the recent Jubilee celebrations makes a lot of intuitive sense.

Of more pressing concern is a weaker sense of identity among those who feel socially, economically and politically excluded. The newspaper preview does not reveal whether this survey also addresses English, Scottish, Welsh and Northern Irish identities.

But there is past evidence of a growing sense of English identity among the white population in England, as set out in a major IPPR report earlier this year. In principle, it could be very worrying if non-white Britons felt strongly included in feeling British, while white Britons rejected it, especially if that was the cause of their doing so. Fortunately, the picture is not that stark. IPPR do report a correlation between those who say they are English not British and anti-politics and anti-diversity sentiments. But the growing English identity is combined with a strong British allegiance for most, while there is a gradual increase in non-white identification with English identity too, but from a lower base. Since almost three-quarters of both whites and non-whites agree that Englishness is not ethnically defined (while one in five of both the majority and the ethnic minorities think it is) means that it is likely that a growing public salience of English identity

will see it continue to become more inclusive, as long as it does not take a closed and exclusive form, which repels allegiance to it. That is an English conversation that is just now beginning to emerge. But this may reflect both the weaknesses and strengths of the recent history of post-war British multiculturalism. It can be argued that – in different times and places – that it had both integrative and segregating effects.

'The claim to British identity can be about a deep sense of shared history too'

The identity evidence on national identity can be used to make the case that, in practice, it proved a route to integration and national identity for many from minority backgrounds. As Michael Ashcroft has reported, it retains a primarily positive meaning for most, tending to mean a commitment to working to make our multi-ethnic society succeed. Yet it has a primarily negative meaning for more white people, tending to be received as paying more attention to our differences than what we share in common, or an asymmetric approach, seeming to celebrate minorities while leaving the majority identity out.

Whatever the merits of that argument, the value of promoting a positive and inclusive national identity that we can all share is that it may be better placed to avoid the risk of reinforcing a sense of 'them and us' than a discussion of diversity or multiculturalism alone.

The good news is that most of us – whatever our ethnic backgrounds – do seem happy to fly a flag for that.

30 June 2012

⇨ The above information is reprinted with kind permission from British Future, a non-partisan think tank. Please visit www.britishfuture.org for further information.

© *British Future 2012*

Chapter 2

EU facts: United Kingdom

The United Kingdom of Great Britain is one of the largest members of the European Union, with a population of approximately 62 million people.

It is made up of England, Scotland, Wales and Northern Ireland, which has a land border with the Republic of Ireland. The national languages are English and Welsh. Britain also has several Crown dependencies and overseas territories, including Gibraltar and the Falkland Islands. Britain is the world's sixth largest economy and has a permanent seat on the United Nations' Security Council.

Recent history

In recent decades, British politics has undergone repeated transformations. The election of a centre-right Conservative Government led by Margaret Thatcher in 1979 started a process of reform marked by the privatisation of many state industries and the rapid decline of the trade union movement. In 1990, Thatcher was replaced as Prime Minister by John Major who continued the same broad programme.

After 18 years of Conservative power, a centre-left Labour Government, led by Tony Blair, was elected in 1997. Labour came to power pledging reform of public services and closer relations with the European Union. Labour won re-election in 2001 and again in 2005. Gordon Brown succeeded Tony Blair as Prime Minister in June 2007. Following 13 years of Labour government, an indecisive General Election in May 2010 resulted in a coalition government between the Conservative and Liberal Democrat parties, led by Conservative Party Leader David Cameron. It is the first Coalition Government to lead the UK since 1945. In recent years, issues of particular importance have included reform of the National Health Service (NHS) and education system, the war in Iraq, and the question of 'Britishness'.

Government structure

Britain is a parliamentary constitutional monarchy. The Head of State is the Monarch, currently Queen Elizabeth II; however, her political powers are largely symbolic. She appoints the leader of the largest party in Parliament as Prime Minister and meets with him or her on a regular basis. Although she has the power to refuse assent to an Act of Parliament, this power is unlikely to be used. Most executive power rests with the Prime Minister, the Cabinet and the other ministers who make up the Government. The Government is answerable to Parliament. The British Parliament has two chambers – the House of Commons and the House of Lords. The first is directly elected while the second is appointed.

Britain also has several different forms of regional and local government. Since 1999 there has been a separate devolved Parliament in Scotland and National Assemblies in Wales and Northern Ireland (although the latter is currently suspended). In England, there are no regional assemblies, except in London, and local government is divided between County Councils and District or Borough Councils. British voters also elect 72 MEPs.

The UK and the EU

The United Kingdom joined the European Community in 1973, following two unsuccessful applications for membership. Since joining, the UK has often had a strained relationship with the rest of the EU, particularly under Prime Ministers Margaret Thatcher and John Major. Having joined the European Community in 1973 under Conservative Prime Minister Edward Heath, the question was put to a referendum in 1975 by the incoming Labour Government. The British people voted to stay in the European Community.

However, when Margaret Thatcher and the Conservative Party returned to power in 1979, they took a more sceptical attitude toward UK membership. This reached a showdown in 1985, when the Prime Minister demanded the repayment of part of the UK's budget contribution. Having won this battle, the British Government played a more constructive role in developing the European project. It was the British Commissioner, Lord Cockfield, who pushed forward the reforming Single European Act (1986). In 1992, Europe erupted as a pressing political issue when Britain was forced to leave the Exchange Rate Mechanism (ERM). A fierce debate also raged about the Maastricht Treaty (1992). The divisions over Europe were so powerful that they nearly caused the collapse of the Conservative Government.

When Tony Blair came to power in 1997, he proposed a friendlier attitude toward the EU. Although Britain showed more willingness to accept EU legislation, the decision was soon taken that the UK would not adopt the Euro as its currency at the same time as other member states. The Government promised that a referendum would be held on the issue. However, there was controversy in 2008 when the Government refused to hold a referendum on the Lisbon Treaty, which was due to come into force in 2009. Despite criticism that the Lisbon Treaty was identical to the failed EU Constitution (which the Government did promise a referendum on) a referendum was denied and the British Parliament ratified the Lisbon Treaty in July 2008. The European Union Bill which is expected to be passed through Parliament in 2011 promises referenda on any future EU Treaty change.

Facts and figures

⇨ Britain is a world leader in services, such as banking and insurance, which account for 72% of GDP.

⇨ Britain is a highly popular tourist destination, attracting 30 million visitors every year.

21 July 2011

⇨ The above information is reprinted with kind permission from CIVITAS. Please visit www.civitas.org.uk for further information.

The monarchy

Information from DirectGov.

The monarch and government

The monarchy is the oldest institution of government in the United Kingdom. The UK's monarchy is considered the oldest of all modern constitutional monarchies (others exist in countries including Belgium, Norway, the Netherlands, Spain and Monaco).

Most powers once exercised by the monarch have now been devolved (transferred) to ministers. In certain circumstances, however, the monarch retains the power to exercise personal discretion over issues such as appointing the Prime Minister and dissolving Parliament, even though these powers may never be used in practice, or may be exercised symbolically.

As a result of a long process of change during which the monarchy's absolute power has been gradually reduced, custom now dictates that the Queen follows ministerial advice.

The Queen performs a range of important duties, such as summoning and dissolving Parliament and giving royal assent to legislation passed by the UK Parliament, the Scottish Parliament, the National Assembly for Wales or the Northern Ireland Assembly.

The Queen formally appoints important office holders, including the Prime Minister and other government ministers, judges, officers in the armed forces, governors, diplomats, bishops and some other senior clergy of the Church of England. She also grants peerages, knighthoods and other honours. In instances where people have been wrongly convicted of crimes, she is involved in pardoning them.

In international affairs, the Queen (as head of state) has the power to declare war and make peace, to recognise foreign states, to conclude treaties and to take over or give up territory.

The Privy Council and other work

The Queen holds Privy Council meetings, gives audiences to her ministers and officials in the UK and overseas, receives accounts of Cabinet decisions, reads dispatches and signs state papers.

She is consulted on many aspects of national life, and must show complete impartiality in the advice she gives. The law states that a regent has to be appointed to perform the royal functions if the monarch is totally incapacitated.

The Privy Council was formerly the chief source of executive power in the state, but as the system of Cabinet government developed in the 18th century, the Cabinet took on much of its role.

Today, the Privy Council is the main way which ministers advise the Queen on the approval of Orders in Council, such as those granting Royal Charters or enacting subordinate legislation, or on the issue of royal proclamations such as the summoning or dissolving of Parliament.

There are about 500 Privy Counsellors, whose appointments are for life. The Privy Council consists of all members of the Cabinet, other senior politicians, senior judges and some individuals from the Commonwealth. Only members of the government of the day, however, play any part in its policy work. The Prime Minister recommends new members of the Privy Council to the sovereign.

The monarch and the Commonwealth

The United Kingdom's current monarch is Elizabeth II. She is resident in and most directly involved with the UK (her oldest realm), although she is Queen (separately and equally) of 15 independent states, their overseas territories and dependencies.

Queen Elizabeth II and the royal family

Born in 1926 (the great-great-granddaughter of Queen Victoria), Elizabeth became Queen at the age of 25, on the death of her father, King George VI. She is the 40th monarch since William the Conqueror.

Elizabeth II was crowned on 2 June 1953 in Westminster Abbey, despite having acceded to the throne on 6 February 1952 when her father died. British law states that the throne is not left 'vacant' and therefore the new monarch succeeds the old monarch immediately. The official coronation usually takes place months later, as it's considered a happy occasion and not appropriate for the period of mourning.

The members of the royal family support the Queen in her public duties, nationally and internationally. Official duties are undertaken by members of the Queen's close family, such as her children and her cousins (the children of her father's brothers), and their wives or husbands.

The royal family plays an important role in supporting and encouraging the public and charity sectors, and around 3,000 organisations list a member of the royal family as a patron or president.

There is no strict legal or formal definition of who is or isn't a member of the royal family, but those carrying the title His or Her Majesty (HM), His or Her Royal Highness (HRH) or Their Royal Highnesses (TRH) are generally considered members. You can find out more about the members of the royal family on the monarchy's official website.

The crown

The title to the crown derives partly from statute and partly from common law rules of descent. Despite interruptions in the direct line of succession, inheritance has always been the way royal power has passed down the generations with sons of the sovereign coming before daughters in succeeding to the throne.

When a daughter does succeed, she becomes Queen Regnant and has the same power as a king. The 'consort' of a king takes her husband's rank and style, becoming Queen. No special rank or privileges are given to the husband of a Queen Regnant.

Under the Act of Settlement of 1700, only Protestant descendants of Princess Sophia, the Electress of Hanover (a granddaughter of James I of England and VI of Scotland) are eligible to succeed. The order of succession to the throne can be altered only by common consent of the countries of the Commonwealth of which the monarch is sovereign.

The sovereign succeeds to the throne as soon as his or her predecessor dies. He or she is at once proclaimed at an Accession Council, to which all members of the Privy Council are called. Members of the House of Lords, the Lord Mayor, Aldermen and other leading citizens of the City of London are also invited.

The coronation follows the accession. The ceremony takes place at Westminster Abbey in London in the presence of representatives of both Houses of Parliament and all the major public organisations in the UK. The prime ministers and leading members of the Commonwealth nations and representatives of other countries also attend.

⇨ The above information is from DirectGov. Please visit www.gov.uk for further information.

© Crown copyright 2012

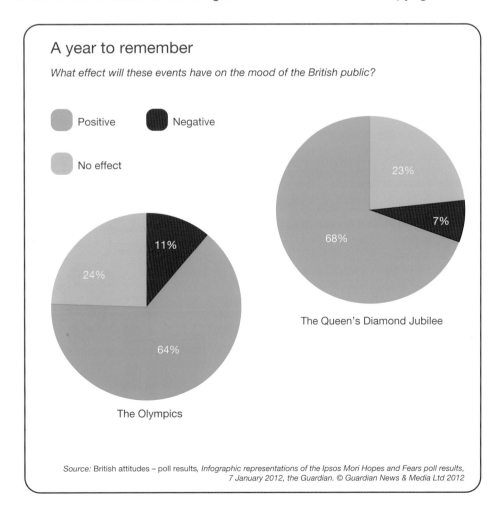

A year to remember

What effect will these events have on the mood of the British public?

Positive ■ Negative

No effect

The Olympics: 11% Negative, 24% No effect, 64% Positive

The Queen's Diamond Jubilee: 23% No effect, 7% Negative, 68% Positive

Source: British attitudes – poll results, Infographic representations of the Ipsos Mori Hopes and Fears poll results, 7 January 2012, the Guardian. © Guardian News & Media Ltd 2012

British identity doesn't need monarchy

As the UK celebrates the Queen's Diamond Jubilee, the 'national' rhetoric is that of a royal Britishness. Peter Tatchell examines the moral and social arguments against this conflation, suggesting the space for a new civic identity via republicanism.

Everyone loves a party. Millions of people – royalists and even some republicans – are enjoying the pageantry and spectacle of the Diamond Jubilee celebrations. I'm glad for them and, as a democrat, I respect their right to laud the Queen.

It is, nevertheless, sad that so many people still seek to express their British identity through the adulation of one very rich, privileged, aristocratic family – the Windsors. Apart from the morally objectionable deference and fawning, the idea that the royal family personifies Britishness is bizarre.

The Queen is descended from German, not British, royalty. In the early twentieth century, they changed their name to Windsor to cover up their Germanic ancestry. Not that I object to German descendants on the British throne. I care not a jot. All immigrants, including royal ones, are welcome. Besides, they've been here for several generations. I accept them as being as British as anyone else.

My sole objection is the con that the royal family's lineage is wholly British and that they, more than anyone else, are deemed to symbolise British tradition and identity.

Moreover, while I see nothing intrinsically wrong with the assertion of Britishness, I can think of more deserving ways to assert it than by celebrating the monarchy and the Diamond Jubilee.

Let's celebrate the extraordinary contributions of British scientists, inventors, explorers, writers, artists, musicians and sports people. I am also immensely proud of Britain's contribution to social reform, from the abolition of slavery to the introduction of parliamentary democracy, freedom of speech, votes for women and the National Health Service. These are, to me, the truly worthy aspects of British achievement and identity.

By contrast, I feel very uncomfortable about the huge resources and significance being given to the Queen's 60 years on the throne; especially compared with the much lesser celebration of the 60th anniversary of Victory in Europe – the defeat of Nazi fascism in 1945.

To defeat fascism, millions of ordinary unsung British people suffered and sacrificed. Many died. Many more were wounded or disabled. They, far more than the royals, represent everything that is positive, noble and inspiring about Britishness.

The 60th anniversary of V-E Day involved far lower key celebrations than the Diamond Jubilee. I remember joining over 100,000 people in central London. I stood there humbled, and in homage, with a simple placard addressed to the assembled veterans: 'Thank you for saving us from fascism.'

We live in freedom, because of their heroism and sacrifice.

The triumph over Nazism is, to me, an anniversary that merits much greater celebration than one aristocrat's six decades as Queen. It symbolises Britishness and British identity in a far more positive, authentic, humane and inspirational way than the Diamond Jubilee.

It is true that Elizabeth II's 60 years as Queen have been mostly harmless and inoffensive. The problem is not the Queen personally. I have nothing major against her. My objection is to the institution of the monarchy. It's a constitutional anachronism; a relic of a long-past feudal, aristocratic age.

An unelected head of state, even a pleasant one like the Queen, is incompatible with democracy and modernity. Monarchy is based on inherited power, wealth and status – not on merit or democratic choice. Deference is enshrined. Equality and accountability are spurned in favour of privilege.

According to the elitist values of the monarchical system, the most stupid, immoral royal is, by virtue of the family into which they are born, more fit to be our head of state than the wisest, most ethical commoner.

These are not the values that I want to see as part of British identity.

Monarchs get the job for life, no matter how appallingly they behave. While the Queen may have done a pretty good job, imagine having to put up with a king like the insensitive, gaffe-prone Prince Philip or the Nazi-sympathising Edward VIII.

Shamefully, we have a system of monarchy that is implicitly racist and based on religious intolerance.

No Catholic or person married to a Catholic can inherit the British throne. The monarch is automatically the Supreme Governor of the Church of England; making royal succession problematic for atheists, Muslims, Judaists, Hindus and Sikhs.

Although not racist by design or intent, the monarchy is racist by default. For the foreseeable future, a black Briton can never be our monarch and head of state. The position of king or queen is reserved for the all-white Windsor family and their descendants. Until a future royal first-in-line marries a non-white person, no Afro-Caribbean, African or Asian person can be the symbolic head of our nation.

The Queen sometimes seems out-of-touch with modern multicultural Britain. She visits many charities and community groups but rarely black ones and never gay ones. The royal embrace seems to have its limits.

For all these reasons, my idea of British identity is separate from the often morally dubious institution of royalty. We do not need to genuflect to the Queen to validate our Britishness. Our identity is not synonymous with royalism.

It is often claimed that the monarchy is preferable to an executive US-style president. However, together with most republicans, I'd prefer to see a low-cost, purely ceremonial, elected president, like Ireland.

This would ensure that the people are sovereign, not the royals. It would give us a very important safeguard: if we don't like our head of state, we can elect a new one. The Queen could stand for election. If she won, which she might, I'd accept the result. Let the people decide.

More information about Peter Tatchell's campaigns: www.PeterTatchell.net and for information about Republic: www.Republic.org.uk.

3 June 2012

⇨ The above information is reprinted with kind permission from openDemocracy. Please visit www.opendemocracy.net.

United Kingdom Parliament

The UK Parliament is based in Westminster, in the centre of London.

It has the power to make new laws and to change old ones and to set taxes for the people of England, Scotland, Wales and Northern Ireland. It also debates the issues of the day and examines what the Government is doing.

The UK Parliament has three parts:

⇨ The House of Commons is where elected Members of Parliament (MPs) sit. We vote for our MPs in a general election. This part of the UK Parliament has the greatest political power.

⇨ Members of the House of Lords are not elected but have been selected by the Prime Minister and appointed by the monarch, currently the Queen.

⇨ The monarch opens and closes Parliament each parliamentary session and following a general election requests the elected representatives to form the Government. The monarch officially signs all the laws that Parliament votes for.

The UK Parliament has devolved some of its powers to other national and regional bodies. In Scotland, for example, the Scottish Parliament has elected members (MSPs – Members of the Scottish Parliament) who make some decisions for Scotland. Wales and Northern Ireland have their own assemblies.

The UK Parliament still makes many decisions which affect Scotland. These are called reserved matters and include defence, foreign policy, the armed forces and the welfare system.

The political party that wins the most seats in a UK general election endeavours to form the Government and, if successful, the leader of the winning party then becomes Prime Minister. The Prime Minister leads the Cabinet and appoints ministers. These ministers head government departments, and run and develop public services and policies.

The UK Parliament website contains a range of information and materials.

6 September 2012

⇨ The above information is reprinted with kind permission from Education Scotland. Please visit www.educationscotland.gov.uk for further information.

The Government, Prime Minister and Cabinet

Information from DirectGov.

Government ministers

Most ministers are members of the House of Commons, although the Government is also fully represented by ministers in the House of Lords.

The composition of governments can vary both in the number of ministers and in the titles of some offices. New ministerial offices may be created, others may be abolished, and functions may be transferred from one minister to another.

The Primer Minister

As head of the UK Government, the Prime Minister oversees the operation of the Civil Service and government agencies, appoints members of the Cabinet, and is the principal government figure in the House of Commons. The Prime Minister is also, by tradition, the First Lord of the Treasury – and draws his or her salary in that role, rather than as Prime Minister.

The Prime Minister's unique position of authority comes from majority support in the House of

Commons and the power to appoint and dismiss ministers. By modern convention, the Prime Minister always sits in the Commons.

The Prime Minister presides over the Cabinet, is responsible for allocating functions amongst ministers and, at regular meetings with the Queen, informs her of the general business of the Government.

The Prime Minister's other responsibilities include recommending a number of appointments to the Queen. Those include high-ranking members of the Church of England, senior judges and certain civil appointments. He also recommends appointments to several public boards and institutions, as well as to various royal and statutory commissions.

The Prime Minister's Office supports him in his role as head of government. This includes providing policy advice, tackling the delivery of government commitments and initiatives, and ensuring effective communications to Parliament, the media and the public.

The Cabinet

The Cabinet is the committee at the centre of the British political system and the supreme decision-making body in the Government.

The British Prime Minister has traditionally been referred to as the 'primus inter pares', which means 'first among equals' and demonstrates that he or she is a member of the collective decision-making body of the Cabinet, rather than an individual who has powers in their own right. The Prime Minister is first among equals simply in recognition of the responsibility held for appointing and dismissing all the other Cabinet members.

Cabinet ministers are the highest-ranking ministers in the Government, and most government departments have one Cabinet minister (or more). Most Cabinet ministers are titled 'Secretary of State' – although some have traditional titles, such as Chancellor of the Exchequer and the Chief Whip.

How Cabinet works

Every Tuesday while Parliament is in session, the Cabinet meets in the Cabinet room at 10 Downing Street to discuss the issues of the day. Government Cabinets have met in the same room since 1856, when it was called the Council Chamber.

The Prime Minister chairs the meeting and sets its agenda; he also decides who speaks around the Cabinet table, and sums up at the end of each item. It is this summing up that then becomes government policy.

Cabinet committees

In addition to the whole Cabinet meetings, a range of Cabinet committees meet in smaller groups to consider policy with other ministers who are closely involved with the relevant issue.

The Prime Minister decides who will sit on these committees, and the relevant committee is consulted for clearance before any new piece of legislation that an individual minister wants to introduce is brought before Parliament.

⇨ The above information is from DirectGov. Please visit www.gov.uk for further information.

© Crown copyright 2012

Devolved government in the UK

The UK is often regarded as a unitary state, but the role of devolved government should not be overlooked.

Scotland

Scotland has a parliament based in Edinburgh. There are 129 members of the Scottish Parliament. They are elected every four years on the additional member system of proportional representation. The current political composition can be found on the Scottish Parliament's website.

The Parliament operates broadly on the Westminster model, electing a First Minister who heads an executive. Its 18 members form a cabinet who manage the £30 billion budget in the areas where the Scottish Parliament has devolved powers. These areas include most aspects of domestic, economic and social policy. The UK Parliament retains control of foreign affairs, defence and national security, macro-economic and fiscal matters, employment and social security. The Scottish

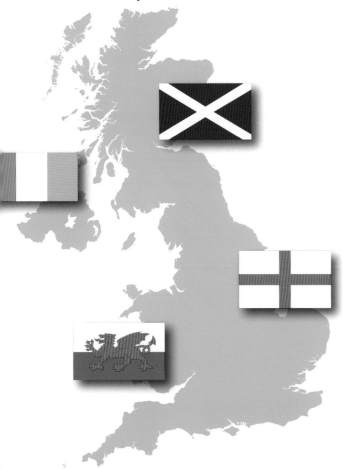

Parliament can pass primary legislation in those areas over which it has responsibility. A list of these areas can be found on the Scottish Government's website.

Scotland is funded by a block grant (decided on the basis of the 'Barnett formula') from the UK Government. Although it has the power to increase or decrease the basic rate of income tax set by the UK Parliament by up to three pence in the pound, it has no tax-raising powers of its own. Scotland's total for public spending is decided in London; how it is spent is a matter for the Scottish executive.

The current Scottish Government is committed to hold a referendum on Scottish independence before the end of its term.

Wales

The National Assembly for Wales has 60 members, elected by the additional member system of proportional representation. The current political composition can be found on the National Assembly for Wales' website.

The Welsh Assembly Government is a cabinet system based on the Scottish executive model, albeit combined with a strong committee system. The current composition of the Welsh cabinet can be found at www.wales. gov.uk.

The Assembly is funded by a block grant and has no powers of taxation. Originally it had power only to make secondary legislation (i.e. orders

and regulations fixing the detail of implementation). Its responsibilities are not as wide as those of the Scottish Parliament: the UK Government retains responsibility for the police and the legal system. The Government of Wales Act 2006 introduced the ability of the Welsh Assembly to make its own primary legislation on devolved matters such as health, education, social services, local government.

Northern Ireland

The current format of devolution in Northern Ireland follows from the 1998 Belfast Agreement (or Good Friday Agreement).

One of the institutions created was the Northern Ireland Assembly. It has 108 members and has a similar range of legislative and executive powers as the Scottish Parliament. The current composition can be found on the Northern Ireland Assembly's website.

The Northern Ireland Executive comprises a First Minister and Deputy First Minister and 11 other ministers. They are allocated in proportion to party strengths in the assembly. The current composition can be found on the Northern Ireland Executive website. There are committees for each of the main functions of the executive. The membership of each committee is again allocated in proportion to party strengths. These committees have scrutiny, policy development and consultative functions.

Since 1999 the executive has intermittently been suspended because of dispute between its first and deputy first ministers and their parties (Democratic Unionist Party and Sinn Féin). In these cases the province reverted to direct rule by the Northern Ireland Office in London.

Asymmetric federalism

There is an element of 'asymmetric federalism' in the UK system of devolution. A true federal system ensures that all the units making up the state have more or less the same powers legally. These are often defined in a written constitution with a supreme court able to settle disputes. But this is not the case in the UK system.

The different elements in the UK state all have different settlements. As a result there is no consistency between the responsibilities of or the models used by Scotland, Wales or Northern Ireland.

English devolution

England itself has no assembly elected by only English voters. Decisions are made by the UK Parliament. However, these decisions can be radically affected by the votes of MPs from non-English parts of the UK. This is known as the 'West Lothian Question', put by Tam Dalyell, MP for that area in the 1970s:

'For how long will English constituencies and English Honourable Members tolerate ... at least 119 Honourable Members from Scotland, Wales and Northern Ireland exercising an important, and probably often decisive, effect on English politics while they themselves have no say in the same matters in Scotland, Wales and Northern Ireland?'

Indeed, there is evidence some of the 1997 Labour Government's bills (e.g. higher education student fees) have passed because of votes from Scottish MPs who themselves, or rather their constituents, were not affected by the measure proposed.

There are calls for a devolved parliament in England (for example from pressure groups and parties such as Justice for England, the Campaign for an English Parliament, or the English Democrats). Although there is a London assembly, voters rejected a north-east regional assembly in a 2004 referendum, meaning English devolution has stalled.

⇨ The above information is reprinted with kind permission from the University of Portsmouth. Please visit www.sshls-dev.port.ac.uk.gov.uk for further information.

© University of Portsmouth 2011

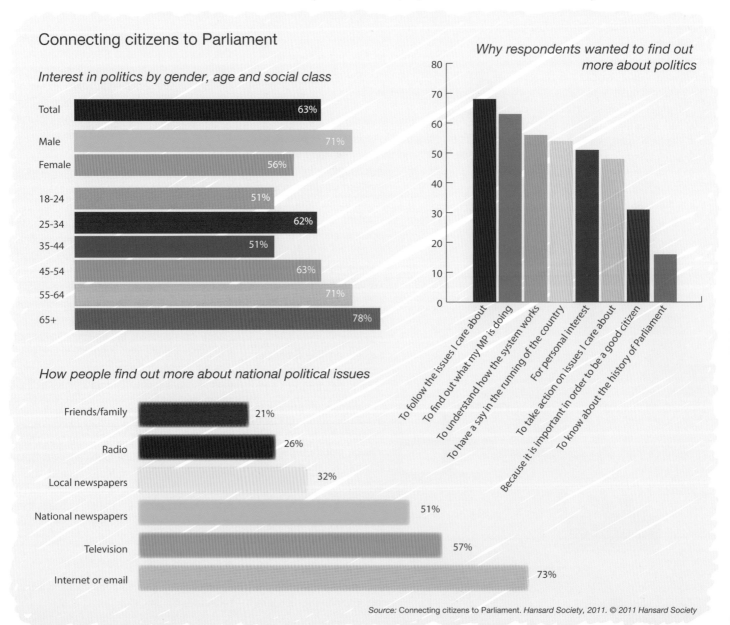

Connecting citizens to Parliament

Interest in politics by gender, age and social class

Total	63%
Male	71%
Female	56%
18-24	51%
25-34	62%
35-44	51%
45-54	63%
55-64	71%
65+	78%

Why respondents wanted to find out more about politics

(Bar chart, values approx.)
- To follow the issues I care about: 68
- To find out what my MP is doing: 63
- To understand how the system works: 56
- To have a say in the running of the country: 54
- For personal interest: 51
- To take action on issues I care about: 48
- Because it is important in order to be a good citizen: 31
- To know about the history of Parliament: 16

How people find out more about national political issues

Friends/family	21%
Radio	26%
Local newspapers	32%
National newspapers	51%
Television	57%
Internet or email	73%

Source: Connecting citizens to Parliament. *Hansard Society, 2011.* © 2011 Hansard Society

Types of voting system	Pros	Cons
First Past The Post (FPTP)		
Current system used in the UK for both general and by-elections. The 'first past the post' label is a bit misleading as there is no fixed winning post, a candidate just needs more votes than anyone else to win. Each voter is allowed to cast one vote, and the candidate with the most votes becomes the Member of Parliament for that constituency.	Easy for voters to understand – one person, one vote. It usually produces a single party government (not the case in 2010 with the Coalition, formed with members of both the Conservative Party and the Liberal Democrats).	Small parties and minority groups may be under-represented as election results are not proportional to votes cast overall.
The Alternative Vote (AV)		
Voters rank candidates in order of preference, indicating their first choice, then their second choice, and so on. Candidates are elected outright if they get more than 50% of the first-preference votes. If not, the candidate with the least votes is eliminated and their votes are redistributed according to the next available preference marked on the ballot paper. This process continues until one candidate has half of the votes and is elected.	The constituency link characteristic of the current First Past the Post system is retained. Voters can put forward alternative choices which can have more impact on the overall result, particularly if their first choice has little chance of winning.	The AV system makes ballot papers more complicated, compared to FPTP.. Smaller parties may find it particularly difficult to gain 50% of votes.
Supplementary Vote (SV)		
The ballot paper has two columns - one for voters to mark their 1st choice and the other to mark their 2nd choice (2nd choice is optional). If no one has the majority, only the top two candidates go onto another round. The 2nd-choice votes of everyone whose first choice has been eliminated are then counted and a winner is declared.	Similar to the AV system, it is even simpler to understand. Likely to lead to majority governments.	Parties may not be rewarded for the share of votes that they gain.
Closed List System (CLS)		
Used in European Parliamentary elections. Each voter has one vote for the party of their choice. Parties present lists of candidates and seats are awarded according to their party's share of the vote. Seats in each region are awarded in proportion to the number of votes cast. This system is likely to produce coalitions.	Often leads to better representation for smaller parties and minority groups. Often a strong connection between votes won and seats gained.	There is no choice of candidates for voters as they must vote for the party as a whole.
Single Transferable Vote (STV)		
Used in Northern Ireland for local, devolved and European elections. When an election takes place, a number of seats will be available in each area, and voters indicate their choice of candidates in order of preference on their ballot paper. A candidate is elected as soon as they reach a certain number of first votes (known as a quota). It is likely to produce coalitions.	Offers voters a choice of candidates from the same party. Fewer votes are 'wasted' (i.e. cast for losing candidates or unnecessarily cast for the winner).	Prone to 'Donkey voting', where voters vote for candidates in the order they appear on the ballot. It is a complicated system to administer.
Additional Member System (AMS)		
A hybrid voting system which combines elements of FPTP and proportional representation: voters in elections for the Scottish Parliament and the Welsh Assembly have two votes – one to elect a Member for their local constituency, and the other to indicate their choice of favourite party. Votes for their local constituency Member are counted using the First Past the Post system. The second vote, for the choice of party, is used to select regional Members. It can make coalitions more likely.	Retains the MP-constituency link. Every voter has at least one effective vote. Often leads to fairer representation for smaller parties and minority groups.	Unlike Proportional Representation systems like STV, results are not as proportional.

©2012 Christina Hughes

For and against: Lowering voting age

Should the voting age in this country be lowered to 16 or kept at 18? Or do you only have enough experience to vote aged 21, or older?

By Daisy Blacklock in Politics Lab

With the next General Election some three years away, we in PoliticsLab asked how members of the public feel about the current minimum voting age: 18. Do they think 18 is the right age to be afforded the right the vote in elections? Or did they think the age needs to go higher or lower?

Discussions over the voting age are inevitably tied up with that small matter of the 'age of majority', or the age at which individuals are recognised as adults in law.

Where some feel that the voting age should be lowered to 16 – the same age at which you can legally marry, have sex, and enter the armed forces in most of the UK, others think that 18 is still too young an age at which individuals can start voting in elections. Instead, some argue that people should be given the vote in their twenties, once they've gained some life experience, are paying taxes, and can think independently.

Back in 2004, the Electoral Commission – the independent body in charge of running and monitoring local and general elections – ran an in-depth study into whether the voting age in Britain should be lowered to 16 or kept at 18.

Their results showed that the majority of those surveyed wanted the voting age to stay at 18. That most countries also set the voting age at 18, and that arriving at a single definition of 'maturity' is difficult, bolstered the argument for retaining 18 as the age of electoral majority.

In 2004, the EC said it would be reviewing voting ages again in five to seven years so the time to renew the debate will surely soon be ripe...

Here's what PoliticsLab participants had to say...

'Funnily enough I campaigned for the voting age to be lowered years ago. I think that it gives youngsters more of an investment in what's happening. However, I also think voting should be compulsory as it is in other countries, for example Australia' Nicy W, Dartford

'I believe that the 16-year-olds that would vote would be a self-selecting, politically interested minority who would add real value to the political discourse' Dan F, Edinburgh

'16-year-olds are just as wise and politically-aware as 18-year-olds' Anon

'At 16 years of age you are able to marry, pay taxes, and leave home. You can legally have sex, which implies it is the age at which the Government deems you old enough to become a parent. If you are deemed old enough to become a parent, get married and contribute to the treasury, then you should be deemed old enough to decide who makes the policies that so greatly affect your life' Anon

'Not particularly passionate about it but I can understand that some 16 and 17-year-olds really want to and are just as informed as older adults (in some cases more so), so let them vote. Most people who vote haven't got a clue about politics anyway' Jon C, Coventry

The voting age should be lowered to 16

'A 16-year-old can pay tax or be sent to fight for their country, but they are currently refused the right to vote for the politicians who can decide how to spend their taxes, or send them off to war' Andrew, Merseyside

'Apathy is the biggest problem facing the UK political system. Engaging people in decision-making at a younger age would help improve this' Anon

The voting age should be raised to 21

'18-year-olds may think that they know everything but they really do not. Unfortunately one does not realise this when one is 18. One needs to have some experience of the world and 21 should be the minimum age – perhaps 25 would be better' Mike M, Gloucestershire

'Because at 18, one is too easily swayed by immoral politicians' R Smith, Scotland

'Idealism turns to reality as you learn and observe' Dave, Wessex

'Even with information on politics at school/college – this seems to be tainted by the teacher/lecturer's bias and therefore cannot be deemed independent. It is evident, based on the school/college location, the 'leaning' toward a particular party. By 21, everyone should be able to use their own experience to decide' Anon

'Extending the period where the person is unable to vote may increase their desire to eventually vote when they hit 21. Maturity is obviously an issue here, too. Though 18-year-olds are getting there, that extra three years (including the experience gained from work, training or university) would be beneficial in making a well-informed decision. Democracy lives or dies on the ability of the electorate to make a well-informed decision, after all' Pete, Bristol

'The younger a person is, the less their ability to make informed judgements, and the matter of government should not be skewed by this factor. The mass student hysteria regarding cuts demonstrated fairly well an inability to see beyond narrow personal concerns' Benjamin L, Holywell

'18 it is too young for them to have much of a judgement on why there is a vote. To them it is more of an 'in the moment thing'. Which party will lower the age of getting a drink, or keep the clubs open, and which won't? Rather than which party will make life easier for the elderly, etc. With that I would also like to point out I would keep the voting age to 18 for the under 21s who join our Armed Forces. With the very nature of the job they are choosing they should have the choice of being able to vote' Jennifer, Wirral

The voting age should stay at 18

'By the age of 18 one has a good understanding of how the country is performing. The UK life expectancy is about 80 years, so at 18 years nearly a quarter of one's life has passed. Therefore, I think one easily has enough life experience by 18 to make an informed decision' Anon

'18 is the age of majority. I don't see any reason to change this. 16 would be far too young and to return to the old 21 would not take account of the fact that by that age many young people are living totally independent lives. The school leaving age is being raised soon. It would be stupid to have people who were still at school being able to vote' Linda E, Leeds

'Having had experience of 16-year-old kids daily, if it's not on an iPhone or iPad, they haven't a clue about the real world' Dave S, Gosport

'18-year-olds are generally aware and intelligent – while some 16-year-olds clearly are far more apathetic or not fully understanding of politics. Since it would be impractical to give the vote at differing ages based on a test of intelligence and political awareness, 18 is an optimal age' Anon, Sussex

'I myself am 21 years of age. I believe that my "reasoned" political opinion has formed since my time away from home at university. I think that 18 is an appropriate age, otherwise political parties would make inappropriate commitments to try and win the votes of the young' Anon

'18 is the age of adulthood, of legal independence and of unrestricted activity. Only legal adults should have the vote' Anon

'Apparently, the judgmental area of the human brain is not fully developed until the age of 19 (which might explain why there are so many motor accidents for young men of 17-21 age group). With age generally comes sagacity and deeper understanding without the knee-jerk, emotive reactions most of us have experienced in our youth' Alison, Cumbria

15 February 2012

⇨ Information from YouGov. Please visit www.yougov.co.uk.

Scottish independence: the essential guide

Following the signing of the 'Edinburgh agreement' on 15 October 2012, a referendum on Scottish independence will take place in 2014. Study the issue in depth and learn all you need to know about what happens next with our essential guide.

By Severin Carrell

The issue at a glance

Around a third of Scotland's 4 million voters believe that Scotland should leave the UK and become independent, ending the 305-year-old political union with England. They believe Scotland's economy, its social policies and its creativity would flourish if it had much greater autonomy. A majority of Scots disagree. They believe Scotland is more secure within the UK, but many want the Scottish parliament to have greater financial and legal powers.

Why is it being talked about now?

The argument is now very real after Alex Salmond, the first minister of Scotland, and David Cameron, the UK prime minister, signed the 'Edinburgh agreement' on 15 October which will give the Scottish parliament the legal power to stage an historic referendum on independence before the end of 2014. Salmond is believed to favour October 2014 for the vote but has not yet revealed his preferred date.

Despite Salmond's hopes that a coalition of civil and business leaders could build a coalition to fund and campaign for a second question on greater devolution in the referendum, those efforts ended in failure. The referendum will instead ask a single 'yes or no' question on independence.

What happens next?

Now that Salmond and Cameron have signed the 'Edinburgh agreement', at a face to face meeting on 15 October, the work on transferring the legal powers to stage the referendum has begun. A so-called Section 30 order which amends the Scotland Act that set up the Holyrood parliament in 1999 will be passed by the House of Commons and agreed by February 2013 by the Privy Council.

In spring 2013, the Scottish government is expected to table a referendum bill, setting out the question, the size of the electorate – including whether 16 and 17 year olds will be allowed to vote for the first time in a major UK poll, and how much the 'yes' and 'no' campaigns can spend.

Alex Salmond has posed the question 'Do you agree that Scotland should be an independent country?' as his preferred question on independence. Election and polling experts say that is not neutral enough, since people find it harder to reject a question asking them to 'agree' to something. The Electoral Commission could well ask for that to be amended, to make it more neutral.

The bill is timetabled to get royal assent in November 2013, when the Scottish government will also publish a white paper detailing its 'prospectus for independence' and setting out the Scottish National party's vision for an independent Scotland.

In June 2014, the final 16 week referendum campaign leading up to a referendum expected to be held in October would be due to start. Then both pro-independence and pro-UK campaigns will intensify, with millions of pounds being spent on television broadcasts, advertising and rallies.

Alongside all these steps on the referendum, the UK government will be putting the final touches to new measures to give the Scottish parliament the authority to set its own income tax rates, borrow some £2bn, and devolve stamp duty (the tax on house sales), land tax and landfill tax, in new powers that will come into force in 2016 – assuming the SNP loses the referendum.

What are the options?

⇨ **Status Quo:** the UK government in charge of most taxation, welfare and economy.

⇨ **Devo plus:** ensures that Scotland has to raise the taxes it spends while keeping defence, pensions and foreign affairs at UK level.

⇨ **Independence:** giving Scotland full control over all taxes, laws and North Sea oil while keeping sterling and the Queen.

What does it mean for me?

⇨ **Someone born in Scotland:** it should mean a greater direct say over one's government and more political freedom, but also greater economic risks, less security and more differences with England

⇨ **Someone living in Scotland but not born there:** the same as before: every voter in Scotland should be treated equally

⇨ **Non-Scottish UK citizen:** not a great deal, but the UK economy will be smaller, oil and whisky might be more expensive, British identity would be diluted and Britain's status overseas could be weaker

⇨ **Someone outside UK:** Scotland is expected to remain in the EU, so there will be few major changes for tourists or investors.

16 October 2012

⇨ The above article originally appeared in *The Guardian* is reprinted with kind permission. Please visit www.guardian.co.uk.

Big Society
– Frequently Asked Questions

Information from the Cabinet Office.

What's the idea?

The Big Society is about shifting the culture – from government action to local action. This is not about encouraging volunteering for the sake of it. This is about equipping people and organisations with the power and resources they need to make a real difference in their communities.

Throughout our communities there is a great appetite for involvement in local initiatives and people do want to make a difference in their area. What often stands in the way and takes the time is unnecessary bureaucracy – red tape, filling in countless forms.

Our focus will be on making it as easy as possible for civil society organisations to help shape and deliver our public services, making it easier to set up and run a civil society organisation and to get more resources to the sector.

What is the Government doing to help?

The Office for Civil Society, part of the Cabinet Office, works across government departments to translate the Big Society agenda into practical policies, and provides support to voluntary and community organisations. It is responsible for delivering a number of key Big Society programmes, including the Big Society Bank,

National Citizen Service pilots, Community Organisers and the Community First fund.

We have also announced a new taskforce, run jointly between the Cabinet Office and the Department for Business, Innovation and Skills (BIS), that will look specifically at the issue of cutting red tape, and reducing the amount of regulation, monitoring and reporting imposed on charities, social enterprises and voluntary organisations.

In addition, we are committed

to training 5,000 Community Organisers across the country. These people will be there to facilitate local action and give support to groups looking to come together to tackle identified problems.

Our National Citizen Service programme for 16-year-olds aims to instil this culture of active citizenship in our young people – giving them the chance to develop the skills needed to be active and responsible citizens, mix with

people from different backgrounds, and start getting involved in their communities. In addition we will also be encouraging social action by working on a national 'Day of Social Action' and making regular community involvement a key element of key civil service staff appraisals.

What is the aim of the Big Society?

The Big Society is about collective action and collective responsibility. We recognise that active local people can be better than state services at finding innovative and more efficient solutions to local problems. Tax-payers want better value for money, and the Big Society can deliver that.

Whether it is in building affordable housing, tackling youth unemployment or inviting charities to deliver public services, we want communities to be part of the answer to the big social problems of our time.

Where is the Big Society making a difference?

There are already several areas including in Eden Valley, one of the most sparsely populated parts of our country, Liverpool, Sutton and Windsor and Maidenhead which are leading the way.

We are seeing lots of people coming forward in Cumbria to develop a community-backed affordable housing scheme, and in Liverpool to build digital inclusion in poorer areas. The work underway here shows that communities, no matter what their background, all have unique and innovative solutions to offer and are interested in shaping their local area.

But this should just be the beginning. We would like to see the action taking place in these areas replicated across the whole country. We want other forward-thinking, entrepreneurial, community-minded people and neighbourhoods in our country to come forward and ask for the same freedoms and the same support.

What is the role of charities and other civil society organisations?

The sector has an important role in Big Society which is about taking power out of the hands of bureaucrats and giving it back to people so they can solve local problems themselves. We have already announced plans for a Big Society Bank which will use money from dormant bank accounts in England to increase the finance options available for social enterprises, charities and other groups. We are also developing plans to reduce the burdens of red-tape on charities and voluntary organisations and open up new opportunities for the sector to deliver public services.

We have been clear that local authorities should not target charities, social enterprises or voluntary and community groups as easy options for savings.

So how can we get involved?

People can start by thinking locally and asking themselves 'What are the issues in my local area?', 'How could I work with others to tackle these issues?', or 'What are the opportunities for my business/ charity?'

One issue worth considering is our idea to promote the establishment of mutual and co-operative organisation among public sector workers: people who think they can do what they're currently doing in a better way. People can form themselves into a mutual, a co-operative, and bid to carry out public service work in the same kind of way that the four vanguard areas have produced community ideas.

⇨ The above information is from the Cabinet Office. Please visit www.cabinetoffice.gov.uk for further information.

Run your own project

vInspired is a charity that helps young people discover the value of volunteering – for themselves and for others. They offer easy-to-access opportunities and support for young people to get involved with good causes in their communities.

Running your own voluntary project can be one of the most exciting and satisfying things you've ever done. You can make the most of your talents, rope in your mates, do the things you've always dreamed of doing and boost your CV, all while making a difference to a cause you care about.

Starting your own project can be daunting, but there are loads of ways to get help, support and funding to get your idea off the ground. Click here for a list of organisations who can help you bring your ideas to life.

Improve your local area

Liam, (AGE), got funding from vcashpoint to set up his own project in his home-town, Milton Keynes, to promote graffiti and skateboard art. 'There wasn't anything like it in Milton Keynes, so I decided to start it myself through contacting friends who are artists and photographers. Make a Difference, a volunteering project in Milton Keynes, helped me to apply for funding .

'A couple of my friends are DJs and they run a DJing workshop. They don't get paid, and they don't care. They are doing something they care about, and they get a buzz. We've created a regular platform for young skaters and artists to get involved in something they have a passion for and show their talents.'

Start a campaign

Evans, 20, set up an anti-violence campaign with help from ITV Fixers, after his friend, Robert Spence, tragically died. 'I have always wanted to do something for my community and then when one of my best mates got stabbed last year at the age of 17, I thought this was an apt time to get started on making my community a better place.

'The biggest thing I did as part of my project was to hold an event in our town hall, called Veto Violence. It was a combination of performances and a debate between local politicians, young people, policemen and even Robert's dad came and spoke. We had over 300 people attend which just made me feel like it was all worthwhile.

'ITV Fixers supported me throughout the project and even made some films about it that were shown on TV, which helped me both to advertise and to spread the word to the wider public. If it convinces just one person to not carry a knife it will be worthwhile.'

Do more of the things you love doing

Celebrity favourite Trekstock was founded in 2006 when Sophie Epstone, then 24, signed up for a Teenage Cancer Trust trek to Everest. To raise money, she put on a little music gig, and promoted it using her now cult 'I love Trekstock' blue badges.

Since then, Sophie has created more opportunities to indulge her passion for music and fashion. Trekstock has launched its own fashion line during London Fashion Week, toured the UK festival circuit, gained charity status, and attracted support from big names including Beth Ditto, Mark Ronson, Katy Perry, Jack & Kelly Osbourne, The Klaxons and more.

Sophie says: 'I think the reason that Trekstock has worked and grown to such a (little monster) huge thing is that I am really passionate about the cause and also despite obstacles I have never given up on it. It may look big now but it all started with a small idea to hold a little fundraiser for a trek and over time the ideas and the drive grew along with the hope that it was going to make a difference to the charities that it supported. I think that if you have a great idea, however big or small, you must believe that it's always doable and there is always support out there to help you make it grow.'

Achieve your dreams

Lake of Stars founder Will Jameson achieved his dream of running an international festival. Back in 1998, after falling in love with Malawi during a six-months' volunteering in Africa, he went to study at Liverpool John Moores University and decided to set up a club night with his mates. The event was named Chibuku Shake Shake, after the Malawian beer, and went on to win Best UK Club in the Mixmag Awards in 2004.

In the same year, he held the first Lake of Stars Festival headlined by Chibuku favourite, Groove Armada's Andy Cato.

Will says 'I had dreamed and talked and thought about starting something back in Malawi for years. A lot of people and close friends tried to advise against the idea and I had no funds to invest but my mind was made up – I had to get it launched and make it happen.

'It had to start small so we could keep costs down but I can't believe how big the project has eventually become. Over 3,000 people attended the festival this year from all across Africa and the rest of the world. It has been the hardest thing I have ever done but then so rewarding at the same time, I love doing it!

'Headline acts like SWAY, Basement Jaxx and the Maccabees volunteer their time and perform for free, a volunteer team run our London office and we work with volunteers from Bristol to Manchester who stage their own brilliant vinspired Lake of Stars gigs and club nights. Together we produce one of the best festivals in the world.'

⇨ The above information is reprinted with kind permission from vInspired. For more information contact info@vinspired.com or please visit www.vinspired.org

© vInspired 2012

Gap year volunteering

Information from Community Service Volunteers (CSV).

Grace's gap year volunteering story

A young volunteer from Leicester is encouraging other young people to take a gap year in the UK that will help people in need, showing that volunteering has the power to change lives and teach new skills.

Grace Tadd, 19, made the brave decision to move away from home to Lancaster and volunteer full-time after leaving college, through UK volunteering charity CSV.

Grace wanted to do something worthwhile with her year away from education.

She was pointed in CSV's direction by her mother, who also volunteered through the charity when she was 18.

Grace now assists a student at Lancaster University who is a wheelchair user, by helping him with dressing, cooking and cleaning, and settling into university life.

Speaking about living away from home, Grace says: 'I didn't know what to expect – this was the first time I had moved away from home and I didn't know anyone. For a little while I felt homesick, but as I got to know people and made new friends I got a lot more comfortable. I feel like Lancaster is my home now!'

After completing her volunteering in June, Grace hopes to go back to college to study Health and Social care. 'Volunteering will help me with my career, and has also given me the experience of spending nearly a year away from home. I have gained independence through looking after myself, and maturity through caring for someone else.'

Grace's mum, Libby, now 49, volunteered in 1980 with CSV at the age of 18. Libby had left school without finishing her A-Levels and decided to volunteer when she found herself stuck in an office job which she didn't like.

Libby says: 'I was placed at a residential school for mentally and physically disabled children called Meldreth Manor near Cambridge. I worked six days a week, helping both the house parents and teachers across the whole age range of five to 18 years.'

Libby says of the experience: 'It was one of the happiest, most fulfilling years I can remember. I was there for a whole academic year and absolutely loved the entire experience – the children, the friends I made, the staff. They even taught me sign language.'

During her year there she applied to do her nurse training, and then went on to train as a sick-children's nurse. Libby is now a specialist nurse working with adults and children with bleeding disorders.

Young people are given the opportunity to work on exciting projects supporting homeless people, socially excluded people, disabled people, elderly people and others. Volunteers can start their six to 12 month placement at any time during the year.

Full-time volunteers are aged 18-35 years. For more information on gap year volunteering, look at CSV's website at www.csv.org.uk/gapyear or call 0800 374 991.

Hannah's gap year volunteering story

Hannah Scotten from King's Lynn dropped out of school in the lower sixth form. She always had an ambition to care for people, but was not sure what career she wanted to pursue.

Her sister, a former CSV full-time volunteer, suggested that she try volunteering with CSV. She then spent her gap year supporting a student with physical disabilities to go to Coventry University.

She now works full-time for CSV – first with CSV Vocal, which helps to support adults with learning disabilities to volunteer in their communities, and now with the CSV Healthy Ageing project, recruiting volunteers to encourage older people to look after their health and well-being.

She says: 'Spending my gap year volunteering gave me the opportunity to find out what I really wanted to do.

'I was drawn back to working for CSV because I knew from being a volunteer that they have an amazing ethos. Anyone can volunteer and everyone has something to give.

'I am now building a career. It's more than just a job, and without my volunteering experience I don't think I would have achieved this much.'

The person that Hannah supported in Coventry now works for UK disability charity Scope.

⇨ The above information is reprinted with kind permission from Community Service Volunteers (CSV). Please visit www.csv.org.uk.

© 2012 CSV

What is The Duke of Edinburgh's Award all about?

A DofE programme is a real adventure from beginning to end.

It doesn't matter who you are or where you're from. You just need to be aged between 14 and 24 and realise there's more to life than sitting on a sofa watching life pass you by.

Levels

You can do programmes at three levels, which when completed, lead to a Bronze, Silver or Gold Duke of Edinburgh's Award.

Sections

You achieve your Award by completing a personal programme of activities in four sections (five if you're going for Gold) – Volunteering, Physical, Skills, Expedition and for Gold, a Residential.

You'll find yourself helping people or the community, getting fitter, developing skills, going on an expedition and taking part in a residential activity (Gold only).

The best bit is – you get to choose what you do!

Your programme can be full of activities and projects that get you buzzing, and along the way you'll pick up experiences, friends and talents that will stay with you for the rest of your life.

If you need any further information, talk to your DofE Leader or, if you're not sure where you can do your DofE, get in touch with your nearest Licensed Organisation and they'll be able to help you!

If you've decided to do your DofE, then find out more info on getting started, choosing your activities and how to complete your DofE and achieve your Award!

If you're still not sure, take a look at why other people think you should do it!

How do I get started?

So you're interested in starting your own programme and achieving an Award? Congratulations, you're about to start an adventure you'll never forget!

First stop is to find your nearest DofE centre. It may be in your school, college, youth group or company. If you're not sure, when you've finished looking around this site, get in touch with your local Licensed Organisation.

Once you've found your centre you'll need to complete an enrolment form and pay a small DofE participation fee (plus possibly a small extra charge for admin and support, added by the DofE centre – they should tell you what this is). Congratulations, you're now a DofE participant!

What happens next?

You will receive a Welcome Pack with lots of helpful info and your Cotswold discount card.

eDofE is where you log your progress through your DofE programme, and is what your Leader checks and approves when you've completed your activity in each section.

When you achieve your Award you'll receive a badge and certificate. You can also use your evidence in eDofE to create an Achievement Pack.

Now, you can start choosing what activities you want to do – although you don't have to wait until you get your Welcome Pack before you start planning your programme.

Remember – tell your Leader about your plans so you don't waste time on activities which won't count or don't fit into the right section. Once everything is agreed and in place you're ready to start your adventure. Good luck and have fun!

Key findings:

⇨ 90% of young people said doing their DofE has given them opportunities to help others.

⇨ 82% noted their DofE has made them want to continue with volunteering/ voluntary activities.

⇨ 62% feel that doing their DofE has helped them make a positive difference to their local community.

⇨ 74% of young people said they developed self-esteem.

⇨ 64% feel that as a result of DofE they are better at sport or physical activity.

⇨ 74% of young people said it allowed them to try activities they would never have tried before.

⇨ 71% of young people identified improved self-belief.

⇨ Three quarters of young people think their DofE Leaders are inspirational.

⇨ The above information is reprinted with kind permission from The Duke of Edinburgh's Award. Please visit www.dofe.org.

© The Duke of Edinburgh's Award 2012

UK Youth Parliament manifesto

The UK Youth Parliament (UKYP) enables young people to use their energy and passion to change the world for the better. Run by young people for young people, UKYP provides opportunities for 11-18-year-olds to use their voice in creative ways to bring about social change.

The UK Youth Parliament has over 600 representatives (369 seats for elected MYPs (Members of Youth Parliament) and over 230 Deputy MYPs, all aged 11-18.

MYPs are usually elected in annual youth elections throughout the UK. Any young person aged 11-18 can stand or vote. In the past two years one million young people have voted in UK Youth Parliament elections.

Once elected MYPs organise events and projects, run campaigns and influence decision-makers on the issues which matter most to young people. All MYPs have the opportunity to meet once a year at the UK Youth Parliament Annual Sitting.

UK Youth Parliament manifesto statements 2011–2012

No to tuition fees, yes to graduate tax

We don't support the system of university tuition fees. We instead support a graduate contribution, in which a graduate would pay a percentage of their salary after they finish higher education (depending on how much they are earning) for a set period of time. This would mean that the total contribution a person makes is linked to the benefit they obtain from higher education. This system would ensure young people are not leaving university saddled with a lifetime of debt.

A curriculum to prepare us for life

We believe that the place of citizenship education in the curriculum should be radically overhauled through a youth-led UK-wide review. Teaching staff should be specifically trained to a national standard to deliver citizenship education following this review. The review should explore the meaning and scope of 'citizenship' along the following lines:

Political education: Young people should be taught the basics of democracy and their rights and roles in society through an impartial political education.

⇨ Sex and Relationships Education (SRE): Every young person across the UK should receive the same high-level standard of SRE in schools. Young people should get SRE from either teachers qualified in this specific field or health professionals. We encourage third-party organisations to deliver relevant sessions in schools and colleges. SRE should have a weekly place in the lesson timetable. SRE needs to include information on both the physical and emotional aspects of relationships.

⇨ Cultural awareness: The curriculum should aim to promote equality, diversity, and an awareness and understanding of special educational needs. The syllabus should include basic sign language skills.

⇨ Community cohesion: The curriculum should encourage young people to make a positive difference within our communities through volunteering.

⇨ Finance skills: There needs to be compulsory financial education within the curriculum. This should give young people practical advice on managing their money, for example information on the processes involved in opening bank accounts and applying for a mortgage. This will help students prepare for later life.

⇨ Sustainable living: There needs to be a place within the curriculum for young people to learn about how they can live sustainably, and adapt their lifestyle in order to conserve natural resources and look after the planet.

⇨ Citizenship Education Test: We believe there should be a standard citizenship test in schools within the citizenship curriculum. This would reflect the test that non-UK Citizens have to complete in order to receive British citizenship.

Independent health clinics in schools

We need health clinics available in every school to provide free and confidential care, treatment and advice for students. These clinics should promote ways to help keep students healthy such as healthy eating.

We believe it must be made clear to young people that it is their legal right to be able to use these services 'in confidence', which means the nurse or health worker will not talk about what students have said to other people such as teachers, without permission, unless they feel that the young person or others need safeguarding from danger.

Better work experience and careers advice

We believe that all young people, between the ages of 13 and 18, should have the opportunity to participate in work experience, in an external working environment, for a minimum of one week in a field of their choice.

Each school should ensure all students can access a professionally trained careers adviser, or make use of external services such as Connexions, for impartial and personalised careers advice. Careers advice services should also do targeted work to engage those not in education, employment or training.

Advertising volunteering opportunities in accessible places

We believe that a broad range of volunteering opportunities for young people need to be more widely advertised both online and offline so young people can positively contribute to their communities.

Young people in control of all youth budgets

There should be more information and advice about ways that young people can get involved in youth budgets to ensure money is spent on the things young people want and need. Decisions made about spending youth budgets should be youth-led.

No change to EU relationship without a referendum

We believe in the principle of the United Kingdom's membership of the European Union. We believe the European Union should open up to more democratic and transparent practices. Any future changes in the relationship between the UK and the European Union, including the adoption of the Euro, should be approved through a referendum.

Proud to be British

We believe that British nationalism should celebrate both our individual identities and beliefs and our unity. We believe that everyone should unite around a collective British identity to create a more harmonious and connected society.

Votes for 16 and 17-year-olds in all public elections.

We believe that 16 and 17-year-olds are long overdue the right to vote in public elections in the UK.

Equal treatment in finance for young people

We believe that personal financial services, for example banks, building societies and insurance companies, should give equal treatment to young people in their service. Retail finance staff should be trained to give

sufficient support and advice to young people when they are using their service. Young people should receive finance skills education within the curriculum so they know not to put up with poor products or bad customer service.

A written UK constitution based on human rights

We believe that the UK should have a written constitution to protect our citizens' rights and codify our political system. This would give the judiciary a fair base to make decisions from, and it could also be used to regulate military intervention by the UK.

Involve young people in the political system

We believe that before young people reach the voting age they should be thoroughly involved in our democracy through a series of measures, such as youth elections, referendums for young people, youth committees, and conferences and events for young people on political issues. We believe there needs to be a legal obligation on both MPs and local authorities to involve young people in decision-making. Such measures would both inform and educate young people and give them practical experience of politics.

A free press that acts legally and morally

We believe that the UK press should have the freedom to publish any material as long as the information

published has been retrieved in a legal and moral manner.

We believe that the press should give a fairer representation to different aspects of our society and report on issues in a balanced way.

Widening access to senior public office

We believe that there needs to be legislation and a sharing of good practice to widen participation and improve the diversity and representativeness of people who take public offices in positions within the UK Parliament, the devolved assemblies, the public sector, the legal sector, the private sector and the voluntary sector.

UK Youth Parliament is for everyone

There are lots of ways for young people everywhere to get involved with the UK Youth Parliament, from supporting our campaigns to debating in our online forums. Maybe you even want to become an MYP yourself!

2011-2012

⇨ Information from the UK Youth Parliament. Please visit www. ukyouthparliament.org.uk for further information and to view the full 2011-2012 manifesto.

© UK Youth Parliament

Key facts

⇨ Citizenship education is about enabling people to make their own decisions and to take responsibility for their own lives and their communities. (page 1)

⇨ 38 percent of people believe that people born outside of the UK have had a positive effect on premier league football. (page 2)

⇨ 66 percent of people believe that people born outside of the UK have had a negative effect on the availability of jobs. (page 2)

⇨ The United Kingdom entered the European Union in 1973. It has a population of 61.7 million. (page 3)

⇨ The United Kingdom is a constitutional monarchy and parliamentary democracy. There is a Scottish parliament in Edinburgh and a Welsh Assembly in Cardiff. (page 3)

⇨ The English account for more than 80% of the UK population. The Scots make up nearly 10% and the Welsh and Northern Irish most of the rest. (page 3)

⇨ 84% of English respondents, 82% of Welsh and 80% of Scottish, associate the Union Jack flag with the monarchy. Around two in five Scottish respondents associate it with democracy and tolerance, compared to over half of the English, and just under half of the Welsh. (page 4)

⇨ 75% of English people associate the Union Jack flag with Team GB. (page 5)

⇨ 70% of people living in the UK and born outside of Britain, feel 'strongly' that they belong to Britain. (page 5)

⇨ 72% of white people in England feel strongly English, compared to 62% of ethnic minorities. (page 6)

⇨ More than three quarters of English people agree with the statement 'I am proud to be a British citizen', compared to just 61% of Scottish people. (page 8)

⇨ 80% of people surveyed believe that the Olympics have been good for British mood. Before the Olympics actually took place, just 53% of people surveyed thought this would be the case. (page 9)

⇨ 75% of people believe that the Olympics showed Britain to be a confident, multi-ethnic society. (page 9)

⇨ 11% of Team GB were born outside of Great Britain. (page 10)

⇨ Two out of five people questioned by YouGov on behalf of the Extremis Project, said they would support politicians who promised to curb all immigration. (page 11)

⇨ 72% of the UK population was born in England, and 11% were born outside the UK. (page 15)

⇨ 55% of Britons would be concerned if a mosque was built in their area. (page 17)

⇨ Only 28% of Britons believe Muslims want to integrate into British society. (page 17)

⇨ The monarchy is the oldest institution of government in the UK. (page 22)

⇨ 63% of people claim to be interested in politics, with over 70% using the Internet or email to find out about political issues. (page 28)

⇨ 39 per cent of those surveyed in the UK agreed Scotland should have independence. (page 32)

⇨ 82% people who took part in a Duke of Edinburgh scheme, noted their DofE made them want to continue with volunteering/voluntary activities. (page 37)

⇨ 62% of people who took part in a Duke of Edinburgh scheme, feel that doing their DofE has helped them make a positive difference to their local community. (page 37)

⇨ The UK Youth Parliament has over 600 representatives (369 seats for elected MYPs (Members of Youth Parliament) and over 230 Deputy MYPs, all aged 11-18. (page 38)

Citizenship (education)

A citizen is an inhabitant of a city, town or country. The concept of citizenship indicates that a person feels as though they are a member of the society in which they live, and that they conduct themselves in a way that is responsible and respectful to fellow citizens.

Ethnic minority

A group of people who are different in their ancestry, culture and traditions from the majority of the population.

European Union (EU)

The European Union (EU) is a group of countries, whose governments work together to improve the way people live in Europe. It was formed in 1957, with just six members, and has grown to include 27 countries. In order to become members, countries are required to pay money (usually in the form of taxes) and agree to follow a set of rules/guidelines.

Government

UK Government is responsible for managing the country. Our Government decides how our taxes are spent, and there are different departments that run different things; the Department of Health, the Department of Education, etc. UK Government is run by the political party with the greatest representation in the House of Commons and is led by the Prime Minister.

Immigration

To immigrate is to move permanently from your home country, and settle somewhere else.

Parliament

Parliament in the UK is different from the Government. Parliament doesn't decide how to run the country, but does approve/change the country's laws and review how the Government is spending our money.

Patriotism

Feeling love and devotion towards your country and its values/beliefs.

Nationalism

Nationalism is often considered to be more aggressive than patriotism, implying the desire to be a completely separate nation and intolerance of influences from other cultures. For example, a Welsh patriot might feel proud to be Welsh and love their country's culture and values, but still be happy to be a part of the United Kingdom.

A Welsh nationalist might feel that Wales should be separate from the UK, and feel intolerant of people or things from outside their country.

Manifesto

A manifesto is usually produced by a political party, and sets out their policy, beliefs and aims in a public document.

Monarchy

A Monarchy is a form of government that has a monarch as the head of state.

Team GB

The team of Olympic Athletes who represented Great Britain in the 2012 Olympic Games.

Assignments

1. What is citizenship and why should it be taught in schools? In small groups, design a poster that includes your definition of citizenship, what should be taught, and why.

2. Look at the graph 'Immigration and integration' on page two. Choose one of the categories for which the majority believe that people born outside of the UK have had a positive effect, e.g. TV. Decide on a well-known, influential person who fits into your chosen category and research their career. Using no more than two sides of paper, write a biography of their life and achievements.

3. Design a leaflet explaining key facts about the UK. You should mention the countries that make up the United Kingdom, its population, its Government, and any other facts you think are important.

4. Think about your local community. This could be your town, your village, your neighbourhood or even your school. How strongly do you feel you belong to that community? Plan an event that will help improve your community's sense of belonging. This could be a street party, a festival or even a volunteering project. Write a plan explaining what your event will be, why you chose that event and how you will get people involved. Will you make posters and flyers? How about a Facebook group? Is your event big enough to need a website? There are lots of options, so be creative.

5. In pairs, prepare a debate in which one of you argues for Scottish independence and the other argues against. Present your debate to the class.

6. Read 'Citizenship test to be rewritten by the Government' on page seven. Write your own citizenship test for those wanting to become British citizens. When you've finished, test your friends and family and see how well they do!

7. Choose a country that is part of the United Kingdom. Prepare a PowerPoint presentation that demonstrates the culture and traditions of that country. You could think about national landmarks, traditional recipes, dress, the country's flag, etc.

8. Do you think the Olympics and the Jubilee had a positive effect on morale in the UK? Discuss in pairs, and think about the reasons behind your opinion. Feed back to the class.

9. Read the article 'How to be British' on page 14. The article is written with a tongue-in-cheek tone, making fun of things that are typically British. Rewrite the article using your own examples of typically British behaviour.

10. Visit the website www.createmyuk.org and play the game that allows you to become Prime Minister. You will choose your Cabinet, pass laws and get creative with your country! Write a few paragraphs summarising what you learned. Are there any improvements that could be made to the game? Was it successful in teaching you more about how the country is run?

11. Read the article 'For and against: Lowering voting age' on page 30. Write a column for your local newspaper, putting forward your point of view: should the voting age in the UK be lowered to 16, raised to 21 or remain at 18?

12. Imagine that you have been asked by Community Service Volunteers (CSV) to design an email advertising campaign that will be sent to students who are considering taking a gap year. Your email should persuade British students to stay at home in the UK for their gap year, volunteering with CSV, instead of volunteering abroad. Use the article on page 36, and the CSV website www.csv.org.uk to help you design your campaign.

13. Read the UK Youth Parliament manifesto on pages 38 and 39. Choose one of their mission statements, such as 'Better work experience and careers advice' and write a letter to your local MYP either agreeing or disagreeing with their view.

14. Research volunteering schemes in your local community. Choose a scheme that takes your interest and imagine that you have been asked to visit your school and do a presentation in assembly that will encourage young people to get involved. You could use PowerPoint, images, video or handouts to help you. Perform your presentation to the rest of the class.

15. Research the government of a country outside of the EU. How does your chosen country decide its laws? Does their government work differently from the UK government? Write a report summarising your findings.

Acknowledgements

The publisher is grateful for permission to reproduce the following material.

While every care has been taken to trace and acknowledge copyright, the publisher tenders its apology for any accidental infringement or where copyright has proved untraceable. The publisher would be pleased to come to a suitable arrangement in any such case with the rightful owner.

Chapter One: Identity and belonging

What is citizenship education? © Citizenship Foundation 2012, *United Kingdom: facts* © European Union, 1995-2012, *What does the Union Jack mean to you?* © 2000-2012 YouGov plc, *(Dis)united kingdom?* © British Future 2012, *Citizenship test to be rewritten by the Government* © The Independent, *Regional nationalism* © Demos 2011, *Have the Olympics ushered in a new, positive Britain?* © British Future 2012, *Let's peel the 'plastic' label off Team GB's foreign-born athletes* © AOL (UK) Limited 2012, *Half of UK voters want 'British values' prioritised* © The Jewish Chronicle, *Identity crisis: are we becoming a disunited kingdom?* © Guardian News & Media Ltd 2012, *What does Britishness mean to you?* © Guardian News & Media Ltd 2012, *How to be British* © HelloGiggles 2012, *How diverse is the UK?* © 2012 Institute for Social & Economic Research, *Muslims are well-integrated in Britain – but no one seems to believe it* © Guardian News & Media Ltd 2012, *Why do non-white Brits feel that little bit more British?* © British Future 2012.

Chapter Two: UK politics

EU facts: United Kingdom © CIVITAS: The Institute for the Study of Civil Society, *The monarchy* © Crown copyright 2012, *British identity doesn't need monarchy* © openDemocracy Ltd. 2012, *United Kingdom Parliament* © Crown copyright 2012, *The Government, Prime Minister and Cabinet* © Crown copyright 2012, *Devolved government in the UK* © University of Portsmouth 2011, *Types of voting system* © 2012 Christina Hughes, *For and against: Lowering voting age* © 2000-2012 YouGov plc, *Scottish independence the essential guide* © Guardian News and Media Ltd 2012.

Chapter Three: Getting involved

Big Society – Frequently Asked Questions © Crown copyright 2012, *Run your own project* © vInspired 2012, *Gap year volunteering* © 2012 CSV, *What is The Duke of Edinburgh's Award all about?* © The Duke of Edinburgh's Award 2012, *UK Youth Parliament manifesto* © UK Youth Parliament.

Illustrations:

Pages 19 and 39: Don Hatcher, pages 1 and 24: Simon Kneebone, pages 3 and 33: Angelo Madrid.

Images:

Cover and pages i, 4 and 13 © dutourdumonde, page 6 © jayeandd, page 13 © Theresa Tibbetts, page 15 © freelancebloke, Page 16 © George Daley, page 24 © Liz Hiers, page 25 © The Prime Minister's Office, page 34: © Saul Herrera.

Additional acknowledgements:

Editorial on behalf of Independence Educational Publishers by Cara Acred.

With thanks to the Independence team: Mary Chapman, Sandra Dennis, Christina Hughes, Jackie Staines and Jan Sunderland.

Cara Acred

Cambridge, January 2013

Discussing Child Abuse

Series Editor: Cara Acred

Volume 248

Independence

First published by Independence Educational Publishers

The Studio, High Green

Great Shelford

Cambridge CB22 5EG

England

© Independence 2013

British Library Cataloguing in Publication Data

Discussing child abuse. -- (Issues ; 248)

1. Child abuse. 2. Child abuse--Prevention.

I. Series II. Acred, Cara editor of compilation.

362.7'6-dc23

ISBN-13: 9781861686541

Printed in Great Britain

MWL Print Group Ltd

Contents

Introduction

Discussing Child Abuse is Volume 248 in the **ISSUES** series. The aim of the series is to offer current, diverse information about important issues in our world, from a UK perspective.

ABOUT DISCUSSING CHILD ABUSE

The issues surrounding child abuse are becoming ever more frequently a part of our daily news. We hear stories of neglect, sexual abuse and physical violence. More recently, there have been shocking reports of faith-based abuse in the UK and of children demonstrating abusive behaviour towards one another. We have also been confronted with a surge of 'historic' abuse allegations that have raised the question of whether it should be mandatory for witnesses to report incidents of abuse to the authorities. This book explores the many different facets of child abuse, raising and debating sensitive issues and considering how child abuse might be tackled through legislative developments.

OUR SOURCES

Titles in the **ISSUES** series are designed to function as educational resource books, providing a balanced overview of a specific subject.

The information in our books is comprised of facts, articles and opinions from many different sources, including:

⇨ Newspaper reports and opinion pieces

⇨ Website factsheets

⇨ Magazine and journal articles

⇨ Statistics and surveys

⇨ Government reports

⇨ Literature from special interest groups

A NOTE ON CRITICAL EVALUATION

Because the information reprinted here is from a number of different sources, readers should bear in mind the origin of the text and whether the source is likely to have a particular bias when presenting information (or when conducting their research). It is hoped that, as you read about the many aspects of the issues explored in this book, you will critically evaluate the information presented.

It is important that you decide whether you are being presented with facts or opinions. Does the writer give a biased or unbiased report? If an opinion is being expressed, do you agree with the writer? Is there potential bias to the 'facts' or statistics behind an article?

ASSIGNMENTS

In the back of this book, you will find a selection of assignments designed to help you engage with the articles you have been reading and to explore your own opinions. Some tasks will take longer than others and there is a mixture of design, writing and research based activities that you can complete alone or in a group.

FURTHER RESEARCH

At the end of each article we have listed its source and a website that you can visit if you would like to conduct your own research. Please remember to critically evaluate any sources that you consult and consider whether the information you are viewing is accurate and unbiased.

Useful weblinks

www.actionforchildren.org.uk

www.afruca.org

www.childline.org

www.intothelight.org.uk

www.familyforeverychild.org

www.ni4kids.com

www.nspcc.org.uk

www.paceuk.info

www.politics.co.uk

www.preventionaction.org

voiceforchildren.blogspot.co.uk

www.youngminds.org.uk

Chapter 1

What is child abuse?

Child abuse

What is child abuse?

Child abuse is a generic term describing the physical or mental mistreatment of anyone under the age of 16.

This abuse takes a variety of forms, from serious sexual and physical assaults to mental and psychological ill-treatment.

Child abuse can be conducted by commission, such as with sexual assault, or by omission, as in the case of neglect or abandonment.

Child abuse is a particularly sensitive, emotive and delicate issue, and is widely perceived as a heinous crime by the general public.

Most forms of child abuse are a criminal offence but civil actions may be taken in negligence against local authorities and police entrusted with child protection.

Background

There is a vast range of legislation and common law guidance regulating the treatment of children, but the earliest statutory examples are the Infant Life Protection Act 1872 (regulating 'baby farming') and the Children Act 1889, imposing criminal sanctions to deter mistreatment of children.

Under the provisions of the poor laws, poor law guardians and juvenile courts were given powers to commit children into the care of local authorities.

Modern arrangements for child protection have undergone an intense period of review since 2001.

In particular, the Home Office published a white paper in 2002 entitled *Protecting the Public*, which put forward a number of new proposals relating to child abuse offences, including an offence of 'grooming' and the strengthening of the sex offenders register (created under the Sexual Offences Act 1997).

The new provisions were included in the Sexual Offences Act 2003; the legislation came into force in May 2004.

The Child Sex Offender Disclosure Scheme was launched by the Government in 2008. The scheme, which allows parents, carers and others to find out from the police whether people who have contact with children have a record for child sex offences, is now available across all 43 police forces in England and Wales.

Further reform of the inter-agency approach to child protection was called for following the Laming review of 2003. Lord Laming's report was published in response to the tragic death of eight-year-old Victoria Climbie who was abused and then later murdered by her foster carer and her partner.

Lord Laming recommended fundamental changes to the organisation and management of services to support children and families. Among the many recommendations were the creation of a 'Children and Families Board' at the heart of government, a 'National Agency for Children and Families' and a national children's database.

The death of another child, 'Baby P', in 2007, who lived in the same London Borough of Haringey under the same social care services as Victoria Climbie, provoked a huge public outcry. The 17-month-old baby boy, Peter Connelly, had suffered horrific injuries over many months of abuse despite countless visits from local authority workers. His mother, her boyfriend and a lodger were later jailed for causing or allowing his death.

Subsequently the Government commissioned a further report from Lord Laming which was published in 2009. Lord Laming noted that many of the reforms he had recommended in his previous report had not been implemented.

In 2010, the Coalition Government confirmed its intention to publish SCR (Serious Case Review) overview reports, 'appropriately redacted and anonymised'.

The Government said that the tragic case of Peter Connelly and other high profile cases had 'shocked the nation' and 'prompted public concern that vital information needed to be made available so that agencies could be properly held to account and all the lessons properly learned'.

The two SCR overview reports relating to Peter Connelly were published in October 2010.

A further report into child protection, the Munro Review published in May 2011, concluded that 'a one-size-fits-all approach to child protection is preventing local areas from focusing on the child'. Professor Eileen Munro recommended that the Government and local authorities should 'operate in an open culture, continually learn from what has happened in the past, trust professionals and give them the best possible training'.

Controversies

Although anyone responsible for child abuse of any sort is treated with public opprobrium, the issue of 'paedophiles' and the potential for their rehabilitation and subsequent re-introduction into society has attracted much controversy in the UK and elsewhere.

This is largely because of the highly emotive nature of the sexual abuse of children, resulting from the perceived innocence of youth, the vulnerability of children and social conceptions of these child abusers as evil and beyond help.

Indeed, when it comes to punishment for those convicted of sexual offences against children, the notion of rehabilitation and human rights is confronted by a social desire for punishment and retribution. This is reflected in a rising trend in vigilantism and 'witch hunts' against those released back into the community.

The issue remains a complex one, with the judiciary's sentencing of offenders and government initiatives to crack down on child abuse often clashing with social perceptions of the culpability of these offenders and the appropriate level of punishment.

The public outcry and the criticism of social services which followed high profile cases of child abuse, such as those of Victoria Climbie and baby Peter Connelly, was reported to have resulted in increased numbers of children being taken into care as social workers erred on the side of caution.

Care application statistics for January 2012, published by Cafcass, the independent Children and Family

Court Advisory and Support Service, showed that 8,403 new applications were received between April 2011 and January 2012, a 12.4% increase compared to the same period in the previous financial year.

Statistics

ChildLine received almost 50,000 cries for help from children and young people in the 12 days from Christmas Eve to 4 January, a 19 per cent increase on last year's figures.

Contacts by telephone, email or online chat to ChildLine totalled 48,751 over the festive period and figures show a staggering 50 per cent increase in the number of counselling interactions on Christmas Day compared with last year.

Family problems remained the primary concern of children and young people who contacted ChildLine, accounting for 14 per cent of the total counselling interactions.

However, there was a dramatic increase in depression and mental health-related counselling, which has increased by 103 per cent compared with Christmas 2010.

Counselling regarding self-harm and suicide also increased by 62 per cent and 57 per cent, respectively. This comes as more and more children are now contacting ChildLine online where many feel more able to talk about the most difficult issues. Visits to the ChildLine website increased by 57 per cent last year.

In 71 cases over the festive season the situation was so serious that they had to be referred to other agencies such as the police and children's services, a 109 per cent increase on last year. Around 59 per cent of these referrals were regarding suicide.

Source: NSPCC – 2012

2011-2012: Care application demand has remained at a very high level.

Between April 2011 and January 2012, Cafcass received 8,403 new applications. This figure is

12.4% higher when compared to the same period last financial year.

Applications received between May 2011 to January 2012 this year have been the highest ever recorded by Cafcass for these individual months. January 2012 saw the highest ever number of care applications recorded in an individual month, with 903 applications

2010-2011: During 2010-2011 Cafcass experienced a 4.2% increase in care applications with 9,200 new applications up from 8,826 in 2009-10, which itself saw a 36% increase on applications we received in 2008-2009.

Source: Cafcass – February 2012

Quotes

'Too often questions are asked if rules and procedures have been met but not whether this has helped children. Everyone in the profession can think of meetings and forms that don't actually make a child safer.

'Whilst some regulation is needed, we need to reduce it to a small, manageable size. Professionals should be spending more time with children, asking how they feel, whether they understand why the social worker is involved in their family, and finding out what they want to happen.'

Professor Eileen Munro – 2011

'Agencies are working more quickly to ensure that children are removed from deeply damaging households where many have been for some time and are showing a lower tolerance for poor parenting. What we are seeing is an elimination of drift in neglect cases and a greater recognition of the appalling impact neglect can have on children.'

Cafcass chief executive Anthony Douglas – February 2012

⇨ The above information is reprinted with kind permission from politics.co.uk. Please visit www.politics.co.uk for further information.

Information for adults physically, emotionally or sexually abused as children

An extract from the Abuse booklet written by Dr Lesley Maunder and Lorna Cameron for Northumberland, Tyne and Wear NHS Foundation Trust.

'I think I'm going mad, my moods are up and down all the time, I can't control them. I sometimes feel so angry that I have to hurt myself to get rid of the feelings...'

'I have memories coming into my mind all the time of what happened to me when I was a child. I can't understand why. I've never thought about those things until now... I don't like what I can remember, it fills me full of fear, I can't believe someone would do that to a child...'

'Relationships are a disaster area for me. I can't trust anyone... the same old pattern occurs again and again, especially with men. It is as if my dad was still around and still harming me. I even react the same, always trying to please and pretending there is nothing wrong... what is it about me that causes this...'?

'I keep out of other people's way, I've learned that is safer, but I feel empty and full of pain...'

'I know I don't want to face what has happened in my life so I don't. I drink, take drugs, binge and starve. All of this hides what has happened...' 'I can never say no to anyone, they can walk all over me, do and say what they want. It's only later that I begin to feel angry and it's usually at myself...'

'I sometimes think I'm completely bad and rotten, then at other times I think no it's not me, it's them...'

People who have been abused as children experience many varied feelings. The descriptions above are just a few examples of the distress people may be left with, though having such feelings does not necessarily mean that you have been abused.

This booklet is written by people who have experienced abuse and by psychologists, and others, who try to help them overcome the effects of what has happened.

It is important to note that many people who have not been abused may also experience the distressing thoughts, symptoms, feelings and behaviour described in this booklet.

What is child abuse?

Abuse of children is something which has happened over the generations irrespective of race, class or culture. Only recently have people recognised that it happens and talked about it a little more openly. Society still has difficulty in accepting that child abuse is widespread, so it often goes unrecognised.

There are different ways that children are abused. All of these are serious and affect the child, even if the child may not seem to be distressed at the time.

Neglect

Neglect occurs when the parent or carer does not provide for the basic needs of a child. This can mean leaving a child alone when he or she is too young (or leaving him or her with brothers or sisters who themselves are not old enough to manage). This can leave the child in dangerous situations. It can mean not looking after children when they are ill or not keeping them clean and warm with a roof over their head. Neglect has serious long-term effects on children.

Emotional neglect

This term is used when parents don't give kind attention, love and comfort to their child. They may appear uninterested in the child, and show no affection or care. This can have serious consequences for the emotional development of that child.

Physical abuse

When a child is subjected to violence such as beating, punching, burning, being bitten, thrown around or kicked they have been physically abused. This is dangerous in the short term for the child who may be in pain or whose life may be at risk. It is also dangerous in the long term as it leaves emotional scars and fears which are also very distressing.

Sexual abuse

A child faced with any kind of sexual contact by any other person may have been sexually abused. The abuse can involve forced intercourse, or other sexual acts, it can involve touching inappropriately. It may be a child's presence or involvement with the sexual acts of others, or being shown pornographic pictures or films. This form of abuse may involve family members, family friends, teachers, carers or strangers. It may have happened only once, for a short period of time or may have happened over a long time. Any sexual abuse can lead to serious distress for the child at the time and/or later in life.

Other forms of abuse can be in the form of mental cruelty such as continuous name-calling or humiliation and excessively harsh punishments.

Facing the pain of abuse

It is common for people to try not to think about the abuse because it is such a painful experience. Do any of these apply to you?

Do you try to excuse it?

'It was just his way of showing love.' 'She had too much stress, that is what caused her outbursts.'

Do you make light of it or play it down?

'He bruised me but it didn't go any further.' 'I was only touched, it wasn't full sexual intercourse'..

Do you blame yourself?

'It was my fault, I must have done something wrong...'

What are some of the signs a child shows when he or she has been abused?

Children who are being abused may show signs of distress at home and in school. These signs are not always noticed by others and the child may even be labelled difficult, disruptive or unwell. Signs of distress may include:

⇨ Eating problems – overeating, starving, bingeing and vomiting, etc.

⇨ Toilet problems – soiling, bedwetting, etc.

⇨ Behaviour changes – becoming disruptive or antisocial, stealing, tantrums, not mixing with others.

⇨ Schooling difficulties – underachievement, truancy, overworking at school.

⇨ Emotional problems – fears, phobias, obsessions, nightmares.

⇨ Self-harm – suicide and self-harm attempts, alcohol or drug misuse.

⇨ Sexual behaviour – sexual behaviour that is not age appropriate.

⇨ Physical problems – frequent illnesses, stomach pains, headaches, urinary infections, genital pain, bruising, broken bones.

These signs do not always mean abuse has occurred. They can be found in children who have not been maltreated or abused. But they are sometimes apparent in children who have been abused, or are unhappy for some other reason.

What are the longer-term effects of being abused as a child?

People respond in different ways to having been abused as children. The following descriptions are only examples of some of the possible longer-term effects of abuse.

Relationships

Adults who were abused as children have often been let down by those they trust most. Trust can become a major issue which can prevent them from having successful adult relationships. People who were abused sometimes feel they cannot rely on their own judgements about others. It is easy to see that because they have not been able to rely on those who were meant to care for them as children they feel afraid of trusting those around them in adult life. This can lead to loneliness and isolation. It can lead to fear of strangers or crowds of people.

Because many people who have been abused feel so unlovable they feel they cannot take the risk of letting others get to know them.

Intimate relationships can also be a problem. For people who have been sexually abused, sexual difficulties may occur. This can include fear of sex, confusion about sexuality, no interest in sex and obsessions relating to sex. If people have been physically abused they may feel tense, fearful or angry in response to affectionate physical contact.

Survivors of abuse can sometimes find themselves getting into unhelpful relationship patterns. This can involve becoming the perfect carer, rescuer, or it may be that they allow themselves to stay in other abusive relationships.

Feelings of self-worth

Because they have always not been treated with the love and respect they deserve, many people who have been abused do not learn to feel love and respect for themselves. Particular difficulties can include a strong sense of being bad or unlovable in some way. Some people may have been told that they were no good and may feel inferior compared to others.

Self-esteem and self-confidence can be very low. This may lead to difficulties in saying no to people, problems in making decisions and letting others take advantage.

Emotions

Survivors of abuse describe a range of difficult emotions that they have to try to manage. Many people feel very depressed at times. This can be so severe that they sometimes think about suicide. Other people may find themselves on an emotional roller coaster with massive mood swings. Shame and guilt are common emotions that often sit alongside depression. Some people experience anxiety, fear, phobias, nightmares and may have problems sleeping.

Aggressive outbursts and angry feelings can also occur. It is not always obvious to the person what the anger is about.

Though it is not surprising that people should be carrying a lot of anger it is as if the anger is just bursting to get out. They may feel guilty and ashamed.

Eating

Many people who have been abused have problems with food and eating and may feel unhappy about the way they look. This may lead to compulsive

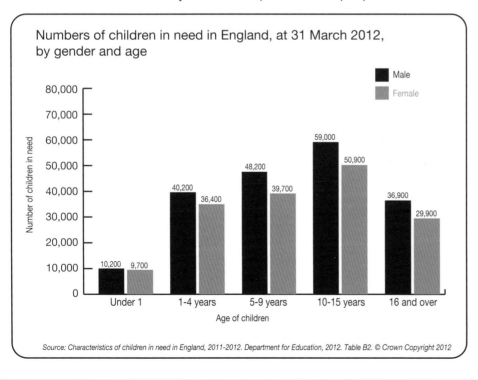

Numbers of children in need in England, at 31 March 2012, by gender and age

■ Male
■ Female

Source: Characteristics of children in need in England, 2011-2012. Department for Education, 2012. Table B2. © Crown Copyright 2012

eating, bingeing and vomiting, or starving.

Flashbacks and nightmares

Many people who have been abused experience flashbacks and nightmares in their adult life. Flashbacks are very clear memories which may make the person feel they are reliving the abuse.

Nightmares can be about what happened or can be about only parts of it, such as being trapped or chased. Both flashbacks and nightmares can be very distressing.

Achievement

Not surprisingly, being abused does seem to have an impact on achievement and performance. Many people set themselves harsh goals and high performance standards. For them whatever they do or achieve is not good enough.

Other people who have been abused do the opposite. They expect nothing of themselves and predict failure. They fear that achievement will draw attention to themselves. They expect that this attention will have negative results such as attack and envy.

Self-harm

Some people who have been abused as children harm themselves in some way. This can be by attempting suicide, or it may be in other ways. Some will cut, burn or injure themselves. Others will drink to excess or abuse drugs. The reasons for this self-harm are complex but often it is used to manage horrible feelings.

For information and advice on how to overcome these feelings, you can read this booklet in its entirety at www.southerntrust.hscni.net/pdf/SelfHelpGuide.10-Abuse.pdf.

Published 2012

⇨ The above information is reproduced by kind permission from Northumberland, Tyne and Wear NHS Foundation Trust. Authors Dr Lesley Maunder and Lorna Cameron, Consultant Clinical Psychologists, The Newcastle upon Tyne Hospitals NHS Foundation Trust. Please visit http://www.ntw.nhs.uk/pic/leaflets/Abuse%20A4%202010.pdf for further information.

© *Northumberland, Tyne and Wear NHS Foundation Trust 2013*

Facts and figures about abuse

Information from Into The Light, www.intothelight.org.uk.

'Support, Counselling, Information and Resources around the issues of sexual abuse for those who have been abused and those that support them'.

What is abuse?

A child is sexually abused when another person who is more sexually mature involves the child in any activity which the other person expects to lead to their sexual arousal or gratification. It is not just intercourse or touching but includes non-touching activities which are sexually stimulating to the abuser.

It is defined by the Department of Health, Education and Home Office in their document *Working Together to Safeguard Children,* 1999:

'Sexual abuse involves forcing or enticing a child or young person to take part in sexual activities, whether or not the child is aware of what is happening. The activities may involve physical contact, including penetrative (e.g. rape or buggery) or non-penetrative acts. They may include non-contact activities, such as involving children in looking at, or in the production of, pornographic material or watching sexual activities, or encouraging children to behave in sexually inappropriate ways.'

Sexual abuse is not new

Sexual abuse like every other kind of abuse is not a new problem. It has been with us since biblical times. In the Old Testament (2 Samuel 13) there is the story of Tamar, a young daughter of King David. Tamar was raped by her older brother Amnon probably age 13 or 14. The resulting chaos that followed led to the eventual death of Amnon and the heir apparent Absalom. Tamar is never mentioned again, but we are left in no doubt that her life was ruined.

How widespread is sexual abuse?

The figures are very upsetting. *Child abuse and neglect in the UK today* (Radford et al., 2011) is a major piece of NSPCC research issued in 2011. The findings of this report show the continuing pervasiveness of sexual abuse in the UK:

⇨ Nearly a quarter of young adults (24.1%) experienced sexual abuse (including contact and non-contact), by an adult or by a peer during childhood.

⇨ One in six children aged 11-17 (16.5%) have experienced sexual abuse.

⇨ Almost one in ten children aged 11-17 (9.4%) have experienced sexual abuse in the past year (2011). Teenage girls aged between 15 and 17 years reported the highest past year rates of sexual abuse.

(Source: Radford, Lorraine, Corral, Susana, Bradley, Christine, Fisher, Helen, Bassett, Claire, Howat, Nick and Collishaw, Stephan (2011) Child abuse and neglect in the UK today. London: NSPCC.)

Tragically, however, the shame and silence often continues into adulthood. As also revealed in the NSPCC study in 2011 was the fact sexual abuse remains a hidden secret, with many children not getting help:

More than one in three children aged 11-17 (34%) who experienced contact sexual abuse by an adult did not tell anyone else about it.

Four out of five children aged 11-17 (82.7%) who experienced contact sexual abuse from a peer did not tell anyone else about it.

(Source: Radford, Lorraine, Corral, Susana, Bradley, Christine, Fisher, Helen, Bassett, Claire, Howat, Nick and Collishaw, Stephan (2011) Child abuse and neglect in the UK today. London: NSPCC.)

Other surveys also confirm the high occurrence of sexual abuse in our society:

In 1991 a survey was carried out by the Child Abuse Studies Unit of the University of North London and revealed that one in two girls (59%) and one in four boys (27%) will experience child sexual abuse by the time they are 18. (Definition of abuse: any event or interaction which the young person reported as abusive/unwanted before the age of 18.)

⇨ 38% of girls sexually abused before the age of 18

(Diana Russell et al. The Secret Trauma 1986)

⇨ 16% of boys are sexually abused before the age of 18

(David Finkelhor et al. Sexual Abuse in a National Survey, 1990)

A study in 2000 (Cawson: NSPCC) also exposes that sexual abuse continues to be extremely prevalent in the UK with 11% of boys under 16 and 21% of girls under 16 experiencing sexual abuse in childhood. In 2008 ChildLine reported a 50% increase in calls relating to sexual abuse since 2005.

In May 2011 the NSPCC reported at least 64 children are sexually abused every day in England and

Wales. More than 23,000 offences – including rape, incest and gross indecency – were recorded by police in 2009-2010, an 8% increase on 2008-2009, the charity said. Girls are six times more likely to be sexually assaulted than boys, the figures suggest. *(Source: BBC website: bbc.co.uk)*

The Internet also has made more readily available images of child sexual abuse.

Sadly, it is not a problem that is just confined to the West. The Bangkok-based international child protection campaign group (ECPAT – End Child Prostitution, Child Pornography and Trafficking of Children for Sexual Purposes) has said that marriage contracts can be found all over the Middle East and South Asia to be a cloak for child abuse. Child rape is also used as a 'weapon of war' in areas of conflict including in 2010 the Congo. In October 2010 more than 1,000 teachers were sacked in Kenya for sexually abusing girls; most of the victims were aged between 12 and 15. *(Source: BBC website)*

Who are abusers?

Research in the UK also shows most abusers are known to the victims.

On TV and in the media, abusers are usually portrayed as strangers in the park wearing dirty raincoats or as men who are members of a paedophile ring. However, research also shows that most abusers are not only known to the victim but related to them. They are not strangers at all. An NSPCC report in 1986, *Child Sexual Abuse Trends in England and Wales,* reported 86% of abusers were a relative or someone known to the child, only 14% were abused by

strangers. This pattern is repeated today.

In 2008 ChildLine reported that 96% of children calling ChildLine because they were being sexually abused knew their abuser.

In 2005-2006 of the 11,976 children calling ChildLine about sexual abuse:

⇨ 59% of abusers were family members,

⇨ 35% were acquaintances

⇨ 5% were strangers

⇨ 22% of girls cited their father as the abuser

⇨ 20% of boys cited their father as the abuser.

Abusers also appear no different to any other man or woman and come from every social strata – builders, doctors, teachers or religious leaders.

D.E.H. Russell completed a study in 1986 (*The Secret Trauma,* NY, 1986) of 152 women who had been incestuously sexually abused:

⇨ 32% of the perpetrators had upper middle class occupations

⇨ 34% had middle class occupations

⇨ 34% had lower class occupations.

There was also no extraordinary racial or ethnic preponderance among the abusers beyond that of the general population.

In 2010 the NSPCC reported that one in four offenders convicted of child Internet porn held positions of trust including teachers, clergy and medical professionals.

Why it has come to light

Child sexual abuse may have been with us throughout the ages, but it has remained hidden, and it is only relatively recently in the UK that legislation protecting the victim has been implemented. Because sexual abuse was not seen it was believed to not exist. It has only been since the 1980s that professional attention from social workers to GPs to teachers have been mobilised to look more closely at child sexual abuse. The ball actually started rolling after a survey was taken in 1986 by the BBC programme *That's Life* asking viewers for their help in an investigation into child abuse. 3,000 adults (of whom 90% were women) completed the survey and 90% of them said they had experienced child sexual abuse.

They also found that children today were suffering as much as had their predecessors. It seems that after this highly publicised media event our society at last sat up and took notice that sexual abuse was happening – and was happening now. As a direct result of this, child care professionals and the voluntary sector established 'ChildLine' a confidential help-line for children.

Today, ChildLine continues to provide help and counsel for children and the statistics around sexual abuse continue to be high. In the 20 years between 1986 and 2006, ChildLine counselled more than 175,000 children about sexual abuse.

ChildLine says 'children often don't tell about abuse because they have been threatened into keeping silent or made to feel ashamed and guilty'.

Sadly the shame and silence often continues into adulthood.

Some positive news though – children are now calling earlier in the cycle of sexual abuse than they did when ChildLine first stated. Nearly 65% of children calling ChildLine in 1986 said the sexual abuse had been going on for more than a year by 2006 that had dropped to 23%.

ChildLine says 'children often don't tell about abuse because they have been threatened into keeping silent or made to feel ashamed and guilty'.

Sadly the shame and silence often continues into adulthood.

⇨ The above information is reprinted with kind permission from Into The Light. Please visit www.intothelight.org.uk for further information.

How safe are our children?

An extract from the NSPCC report How safe are our children?

Overview

Society must be to account on child cruelty

It is incumbent on any society to protect its children from abuse and neglect. So how well protected are children in the UK? As an organisation dedicated to ending child cruelty, the NSPCC believes that not only is it important to understand how many children are being abused and neglected – it is also necessary to track progress if society is to be held to account for its responsibility to children. Only by monitoring the extent of child abuse and neglect in the UK can we judge whether efforts to prevent maltreatment and to protect children are working.

The complex, hidden and multifaceted nature of child abuse and neglect means that it will always be necessary to view the answer through multiple lenses. Child abuse takes many different forms and is, more often than not, undetected. Therefore it needs to be measured in different ways. Each source of data has its own merits and weaknesses.

This report compiles the most robust and up-to-date data that exists across each of the four nations in the UK. We present different perspectives on the question 'how safe are our children?'. We have set out the strengths and flaws of the indicators we have chosen. By piecing together the evidence, we provide the most comprehensive picture yet of how safe children in the UK are from abuse and neglect.

In some ways today's children are safer...

In some ways today's children are safer from abuse and neglect than those of previous generations. The child homicide rate is in decline. Fewer children are dying as a result of assault or suicide in England, Wales and Scotland.[1] Although the

evidence is mixed,[2] it does appear that the prevalence of some forms of child maltreatment is declining in the UK. There has been, for instance, a decrease in physical and sexual abuse in recent decades,[3] similar to trends found in the US.[4]

...but worrying levels of abuse still remain

Despite this, the extent of child abuse and neglect in our society remains deeply worrying. It is an outrage that more than one child a week dies because of maltreatment and that one in five children today have experienced serious physical abuse, sexual abuse or severe physical or emotional neglect. Child abuse is more prevalent, and more devastating, than many of us are prepared to recognise. Take this fact, for example: last year a total of 2,900 rapes or attempted rapes of children under the age of 13 were recorded in England, Wales and Scotland, equivalent to eight every day.

What's more, new kinds of threats are emerging, particularly with the increasing amount of time children spend in the digital world. As many as one in four 11- and 12-year-olds experience something on a social networking site that bothers them almost every day. While parents are used to equipping their children to deal with real or potential threats to their safety, they are much less confident when dealing with the online world.

Child protection services are working in overdrive

In this context, and in the wake of several high profile child abuse inquiries, child protection services[5] are working in overdrive. The number

1 Northern Ireland is the exception – the child suicide rate is increasing.

2 See, for example, Gilbert, R. et al. (2012) 'Child maltreatment: variation in trends and policies in six developed countries', *The Lancet*, 379 (9817): 758-72.

3 See Radford, L. et al. (2011) *Child abuse and neglect in the UK today*, NSPCC.

4 See Finklehor, D. and Jones, L. (2012) 'Trends in Child Maltreatment', *The Lancet*, 379 (9831): 2048-49.

5 See the glossary for a definition of child protection services.

of children being referred to social services has increased in England and Northern Ireland in recent years. Children who are referred are more likely to receive an assessment or be subject to some further action compared with five years ago. Across the UK more children are being considered as 'in need'[6] due to suffering abuse and neglect,[7] more are being made subject to child protection plans or placed on registers and more are being taken into care as a result of abuse or neglect.[8] In addition the public is becoming more vigilant: there has been a 46 per cent increase in the number of people coming forward to report concerns about abuse and neglect to the NSPCC since 2009/10.

The evidence also points to child protection services working harder to reduce the harm suffered by children due to abuse or neglect. 'Drift' in decision making has not disappeared but appears to be lessening as the proportion of children subject to child protection plans or registers for more than two years has been decreasing. More children are coming off child protection plans or registers after shorter periods of time and are not being re-registered, suggesting that risk is being reasonably assessed. The proportion of looked-after children who have had more than three placements has also decreased in England and Wales, suggesting an improvement in placement stability. While there remains much room for improvement, child protection services do appear to be working harder to reduce harm in the context of increasing pressures.

Most children who are abused or neglected are not known to services

However, there remains a significant gap between the number of children experiencing abuse and neglect and those known to services. For every child subject to a child protection plan or on a register in the UK, we estimate that there are likely to be around eight other children who have suffered maltreatment.[9] Abuse and neglect is often hidden from view. Children may not disclose what is happening to them because they fear the repercussions or think that they will not be believed. They may be too young to realise that what is happening to them is wrong. Or their abuse may not be reported even by those who know about it. Whatever the reason, more children suffer abuse and neglect than are ever subject to an intervention by the police or social services. That is why ChildLine gives children a private and confidential place to talk to a counsellor; why ChildLine's School Services helps equip primary school children to better protect themselves; and why the NSPCC offers members of the public a free 24/7 helpline to seek advice if they have concerns about a child.

The gap is unlikely to close

Could services ever reach all maltreated children? Even if this were desirable (and few would consider this level of state intrusion into family life appropriate), it is very unlikely in the current context. If children's social services were to become aware of just one quarter of those children who were maltreated (but not currently known to them), we estimate the number of children subject to child protection plans or on registers in the UK would triple. The resources required for this would be significant: an estimated additional £360 million to £490 million in public spending. In today's fiscal climate this kind of investment is unlikely; to close the gap altogether is highly improbable. Nor is this the most effective approach. While it is vital to support children and adults in speaking up about abuse, in order to stop abuse in its tracks, this will never be enough to prevent children from being harmed in the first place.

We need a different approach to child protection

Which is why a different approach to child protection is needed, one that does more to prevent abuse 'upstream' rather than intervening to stop it once it has already happened. Most public spending goes towards picking up the pieces rather than into 'upstream' prevention. The National Audit Office estimates that only six per cent of public expenditure is focused on stopping problems from emerging in the first place.[10] While intervening to address abuse once it is known will always be a moral and legal imperative, child abuse and neglect will never be substantially reduced unless we become smarter at preventing it from happening at all.

Understanding the circumstances in which children are at increased risk is essential for prevention. Research points to the personal characteristics, family circumstances and environments that place children at greater risk of abuse and neglect. But by recognising that children living in such circumstances are at heightened risk, greater support could be directed towards families to reduce the chances of abuse and neglect from occurring at all. While this support comes at a price, it is ultimately more cost-effective to prevent abuse from occurring than to meet the many costs that fall across society because of the damage caused to children who were abused or neglected in their childhood.

Wider society also has an important role to play. Abusive behaviour cannot be stamped out by the state alone; individuals, families and communities must also be responsible for the change. Most adults think parents, families, friends and neighbours have a responsibility to prevent child abuse – and that greater responsibility lies with these groups than with government.[11] So while government can do much to influence the conditions in which children live and while professionals play an important role in intervening to protect children and helping those who are at risk of abuse, wider society has a responsibility too. However, all too often people

6 See glossary.

7 England and Wales only; breakdown not available for Northern Ireland; data not available for Scotland.

8 The number of children who are looked after due to abuse or neglect has increased in England and Wales in the past few years. In Scotland and Northern Ireland, where comparable data is not available, the number of children who are looked after has increased over the past decade.

9 Calculated on the basis that 520,000 children were maltreated by their parent/guardian in 2011 and 58,000 were on child protection plans/registers in England, Wales and Northern Ireland.

10 National Audio Office (2013) *Early Action: landscape review*, January 2013, p.13. Scotland does better with nine per cent being channelled into early action programmes from April 2012, but across the piece spending is focussed on reacting rather than preventing.

11 YouGov survey for NSPCC December 2012.

frame this responsibility in terms of being willing to act if worried about a child, rather than being willing to address faults in their own or others' behaviour. Perhaps it is time to reassert our responsibilities to children as citizens.

Conclusion

The indicators in this report reveal a complex but compelling story about the extent of child abuse and neglect in the UK today. Despite some improvements in children's safety, worrying levels of child maltreatment still exist. The majority of child abuse and neglect never comes to the attention of statutory authorities and services are unlikely ever to reach all children in such circumstances. While we should always encourage children to speak out if they are being abused, this alone will never be sufficient. Rather than focus our attention on increasing the reach of services already working in overdrive, we should be looking for more

effective ways to prevent abuse and neglect from occurring in the first place. To do this we need to better understand the circumstances in which children are at increased risk of abuse and neglect and intervene earlier and more effectively in such circumstances.

While this report provides the most comprehensive overview of the data that exists, the picture is far from complete. The exercise of pulling a range of data sources for four nations together is akin to completing a large jigsaw, with some of the pieces still missing. Putting the pieces together is not straightforward, since it entails aligning different sources of data which are not always easily comparable. This report has highlighted some of the woeful gaps in our understanding of the extent of child abuse and neglect in the UK. These need to be addressed if we are effectively to hold society to account for the safety of children.

We intend to track progress against the indicators we have presented in this report in the coming years. What would progress look like? We believe that the UK will be on the right track if, in the next few years, deaths due to child maltreatment and the number of children experiencing abuse and neglect in their childhood falls, while at the same time the risk of abuse associated with the factors we have identified decreases. Only then can we be sure that we are on the right path towards ending child cruelty.

April 2013

⇨ The above article is an extract from the report *How safe are our children?* and is reprinted with kind permission from the NSPCC. Please visit www. nspcc.org.uk for further information.

Speaking to your children about 'Stranger Danger'

In light of the awful abduction recently of five-year-old April Jones in Wales we asked local parents, 'When we hear these terrible stories in the media does it prompt us to think about speaking to our children about their personal safety?

'What is the best way to discuss this difficult subject in a way that they won't find frightening? Are we doing enough as a society to make child safety a top priority?'

Ni4kids Editor Nadia Duncan admitted she found it hard to approach the subject matter with her five-year-old son. 'I admit the April Jones case did make me think it was about time I had that conversation. I had always thought he was too young before now. I like to think I always know exactly where he is at all times and who he is with, but there was one incident when he was on a day trip

out with a group and he wandered off. Luckily he was found quickly but he is naturally a really friendly child and I do worry. It made me think that I needed to have the chat with him about not only never ever going anywhere with someone he doesn't know, but to always tell his mummy and daddy everything. It's not a nice conversation to have but, unfortunately, I do think it's necessary. I was really interested to find out what other parents' views on this were.'

Mum April Ross said she explained to her daughter (now nine) about strangers from before she could probably understand it. 'I ALWAYS made her aware of bad men/ women and NEVER to speak to anyone if she was ever alone! I explained what to do if anyone ever approached her in person or by car. She has known her address and phone number, granny's phone number and 999 from when she was

very little. She has been out playing in the street from when she was about four and only in the past year been allowed into the next street where her friends live. She walks to and from school each day (mostly with friends but sometimes on her own), which is a five-minute walk. I always mention before she leaves the house to remember not to talk to strangers! She is a normal, happy girl who loves playing outdoors but understands the dangers of what's out there.'

'I've told my ten and seven-year-old all about the danger of strangers,' says mum Tara Craig 'but you just never know if it's going in one ear and out the next. April's story is a terrifying reminder of the dangers that are out there.'

Courtney Bowers agrees, stating: 'I feel it's never too young to reinforce not going with ANYONE without mummy or daddy's permission.

Give your child the confidence to appropriately speak out against adults – sometimes we don't allow them to do through embarrassment or fear that they will be perceived as arrogant.'

ChildLine volunteer, Alison Ferguson Walsh has more experience than most of discussing these issues as she regularly goes to local schools to talk to children and says she has been getting great feedback. She believes children are more astute and aware than we think.

But is the notion of 'Stranger danger', a red herring?

Alison Ferguson Walsh thinks parents need to remember that their children need to be aware of being safe all the time, i.e. stranger danger is rare compared to incidents with family members and those they already know. It's awful to think this way but statistics demonstrate this.

Sally McCabe agrees, commenting: 'The problem here is the word 'stranger'. All too often it isn't a stranger that is the person they should stay away from. The person

arrested in the April Jones case was known to the family. My children are taught to never go anywhere with anyone without checking with me and that means face to face. I would apply this to other children as well. I don't want them going off with anyone without my say so. If they are lost they have been told to approach any woman with children to ask for help, I know it's sexist but it is something I feel comfortable with.'

Last word goes to Teresa Majury who states, 'I agree with Sally, stranger danger can be a bit of a red herring. Children should not go off with anyone without first okaying it with their parents/carer/responsible adult. We need to raise children who aren't scared to communicate any worries with their parents and to talk through anything bothering them be it bullying, school work, relationships, etc.'

Ni4kids contacted the PSNI for some advice on this subject.

Staying safe online

The following are steps to take that can help to keep young people

safe online and prevent them from becoming a victim of malicious behaviour, crime or fraud:

⇨ Never use your real name.

⇨ Never tell anyone personal things about yourself or your family such as your address, phone number or the name of your school.

⇨ Instead of posting a photo of yourself online, consider using a picture you like or a photo of your favourite band.

⇨ Don't post photos or videos that you wouldn't be happy for your parents or teacher to see. Once online they can be copied and posted in other places where you can't get rid of them.

⇨ Keep passwords private and don't tell anyone, not even your best friend.

⇨ When adding or accepting friends on social media sites, don't add anyone you don't know, even if they say they know you.

⇨ If someone contacts you with weird or nasty messages, don't reply to them but do save the messages. Tell someone you trust such as your parents or a teacher as soon as possible and show them what you have been sent.

⇨ When writing a blog, be careful about what you write in it. Don't include too many personal details about yourself.

⇨ Don't arrange to meet in person with someone you have met online. Some people lie online and may not be who they say they are.

⇨ If someone you are unsure of contacts you on a forum, contact the forum administrator.

Indecent images

Police also want to highlight the risks to those involved in the exchanging of indecent images between children, both on the Internet and by mobile phones. Both the victims and those involved in circulating these types of images may not be aware of the consequences of this type of activity, thinking that it is a bit of harmless fun. Again, young people should remember that once anything is emailed or texted to another person or posted online it can be copied and posted in other places where you can't get rid of them.

There are serious criminal offences committed by those who make, send or possess indecent images of children which are punishable with lengthy prison sentences. Those whose images are being sent around have no control over where they may end up and this can have long-reaching effects on their future, not to mention the distress this can cause to parents, siblings, schools and themselves. Young people involved in these incidents foolishly believed that the images would not be made public and have bitterly regretted the trauma that has resulted from a few moments of madness.

Parents should be aware of their responsibilities in relation to the supervision of their children, especially when Internet access is available to them in the home. Parents may not be aware of the fact that any such images are stored on their computer or mobile phone which they have bought for their child. They may still have committed an offence as the images have been stored or sent through their Internet or telephone service provider.

Internet safety

The Child Exploitation and Online Protection Centre (CEOP) has a website which provides advice to children and parents about Internet safety, how to avoid becoming a victim and parental responsibilities. They also give details about how to report abuse and will investigate Internet abusers. www.ceop.gov.uk

Advice issued by police for parents in relation to child safety on the Internet and when using mobile phones:

⇨ Know what your children are doing online and who they are talking to. Ask them to teach you to use any applications you have never used.

⇨ Help your children to understand that they should never give out personal details to online friends – personal information includes their messenger id, email address, mobile number and any pictures of themselves, their family or friends – if your child publishes a picture or video online – anyone can change it or share it.

⇨ If your child receives spam / junk email and texts, remind them never to believe them, reply to them or use them.

⇨ It's not a good idea for your child to open files that are from people they don't know. They won't know what they contain – it could be a virus, or worse – an inappropriate image or film.

⇨ Help your child to understand that some people lie online and that therefore it's better to keep online mates online. They

should never meet up with any strangers without an adult they trust.

⇨ Always keep communication open for a child to know that it's never too late to tell someone if something makes them feel uncomfortable.

⇨ Teach young people how to block someone online and report them if they feel uncomfortable.

⇨ It's important for parents to remember that many new mobile phones have web access, and more recently mobile TV has been launched. This means that young people can access content from the Internet and TV wherever they are.

October 2012

⇨ The above information is reprinted with kind permission from Ni4kids.com. Please visit www.ni4kids.com for further information.

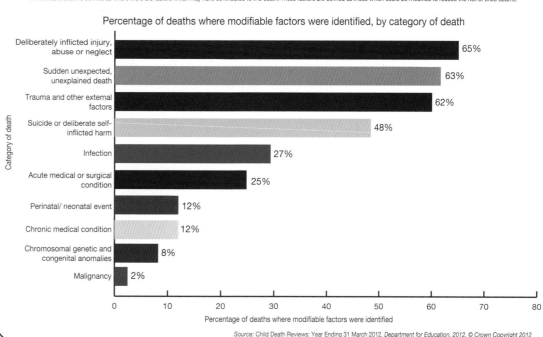

Child death reviews, year ending March 2012

In the year ending 31 March 2012, 4,012 child death reviews were completed by Child Death Overview Panels. This is slightly lower than the number of reviews completed in the year ending 31 March 2011 (1% fewer reviews were completed in the year ending 31 March 2012). Of the child death reviews completed in the year ending 31 March 2012, 784 were identified as having modifiable* factors (20%). This is the same proportion as identified in the year ending 31 March 2011.

A modifiable death is defined as where there are factors which may have contributed to the death. These factors are defined as those which could be modified to reduce the risk of child deaths.

Percentage of deaths where modifiable factors were identified, by category of death

Category of death	%
Deliberately inflicted injury, abuse or neglect	65%
Sudden unexpected, unexplained death	63%
Trauma and other external factors	62%
Suicide or deliberate self-inflicted harm	48%
Infection	27%
Acute medical or surgical condition	25%
Perinatal/ neonatal event	12%
Chronic medical condition	12%
Chromosomal genetic and congenital anomalies	8%
Malignancy	2%

Percentage of deaths where modifiable factors were identified

Source: Child Death Reviews: Year Ending 31 March 2012. Department for Education, 2012. © Crown Copyright 2012

Children safer from strangers in the park than their bedroom, NSPCC warns

Children are safer playing out in the street or their local park than on the Internet, a landmark report by the NSPCC shows.

Educating young people about traditional 'stranger danger' is failing to equip them for new 'emerging threats' on social networking sites and through phenomena such as 'sexting' or cyberbullying, it warns.

Meanwhile the report, billed as the comprehensive study of risks to children in the UK, also warns only a small a fraction of abuse or neglect in the home is being detected.

Only around one in nine of the estimated 520,000 children mistreated in their own home every year is under formal protection plans by their local authority, the charity calculates

Even on official figures, children are twice as likely to suffer mistreatment in the home than outside, but the report concludes that abuse is 'more often than not undetected'.

There were more than 21,500 recorded sexual offences against children in the UK last year alone, including almost 6,000 rapes.

But, overall the report, which pulls together a raft of official data and surveys, shows a significant long-term decline in violence against children in comparison with previous decades, contrary to public perceptions, but major new threats emerging through the Internet.

Child murder, for example, is down by 30 per cent since the early 1980s and serious assaults involving children have also declined steadily as have child suicide rates in most of the country.

But with children as young as five spending up to six hours a week on the Internet, a quarter of 11- and 12-year-olds now see something which worries them on the Internet every day, it warns.

Almost three out of ten of those aged 11-to-16 have been bullied over the Internet or through a smart phone and about one in 13 of them suffers 'persistent' cyberbullying, the charity estimates.

More than one in ten children in the same age group has been on the receiving end of a sexually explicit message – a proportion which almost doubles among those aged 15 and 16. Meanwhile almost a third have had contact with a stranger on the Internet and a quarter of nine- to 16-year-olds have seen sexual images online in the last year.

Greater vigilance in the wake of scandals such as the Baby Peter case have triggered a sharp rise in recorded cases of neglect, but the NSPCC estimates that in reality it is happening at a similar rate to a decade ago.

Lisa Hawker, author of the report, said: 'We are still trying to fully understand the scale of online harm but children are telling us that cyberbullying, sexting and seeing sexual images online are things that many of them are experiencing.

'Parents are perhaps unaware that when your child is using a computer or mobile phone they may be at greater risk of being hurt or harmed in some way than if they are out and about in their local park.

'The changing nature of the way we live our lives means that actually your chances of meeting someone who can harm you is now much greater through the Internet or your mobile phone than through a stranger you might come across in the street or the local park.'

The report remarks that in many ways children today are safer than previous generations, at least from traditional sources of danger.

But it adds: 'Despite this, the extent of child abuse and neglect in our society remains deeply worrying.

'It is an outrage that more than one child a week dies because of maltreatment and that one in five children today has experienced serious physical abuse, sexual abuse or severe physical or emotional neglect.

'Child abuse is more prevalent, and more devastating, than many of us are prepared to recognise.'

It adds: 'What's more, new kinds of threats are emerging, particularly with the increasing amount of time children spend in the digital world ... while parents are used to equipping their children to deal with real or potential threats to their safety, they are much less confident when dealing with the online world.'

The report concludes that it would be impossible for social services ever to detect all cases of maltreatment of children in the home and calls for a shift in policy towards spotting warning signs and prevention.

'Wider society also has an important role to play, abusive behaviour cannot be stamped out by the state alone,' it says.

'Individuals, families and communities must also be responsible for the change.

'All too often people frame this responsibility in terms of being willing to act if worried about a child, rather than being willing to address faults in their own or others' behaviour.

'Perhaps it is time to reassert our responsibilities to children as citizens.'

18 April 2013

⇨ The above information is reprinted with kind permission from _The Daily Telegraph_. Please visit www.telegraph.co.uk.

© _John Bingham/_
The Daily Telegraph 2013

Shock toll of child-on-child abuse

The NSPCC said more than 5,000 cases of sex abuse by under-18s were reported in the last three years.

Thousands of young people are committing acts of sexual abuse against other children every year, the NSPCC warned.

The charity found there were more than 5,000 cases of abuse by under-18s reported to the police in the last three years. In some instances acts of sexual abuse were committed by children as young as five or six.

Nearly all – 98% – of the 4,562 offenders were boys and where the relationship was recorded, at least three out of five of the victims knew their abuser, the NSPCC said. More than a third of the offences were said to have been committed by a family friend or acquaintance, and one in five by family members.

'Thousands of young people are committing acts of sexual abuse against other children every year'

The NSPCC obtained the statistics through Freedom of Information requests to each of the 43 police forces in England and Wales. But only 34 forces supplied figures – revealing a total of 5,028 offences – so the true number of offences is likely to be higher, the NSPCC said.

The findings follow a report by probation inspectors last month which found that police, social workers and teachers were missing the warning signs that a child may sexually offend.

The NSPCC warned that easy access to indecent material could be leading to an increase in the number of children needing help. The charity has found that more children were carrying out online grooming and harassment.

Claire Lilley, policy adviser at the NSPCC, said she hoped the findings would ring 'alarm bells' with authorities that the problem required urgent action. She said: 'In some cases older children are attacking younger ones and in other cases it's sexual violence within a teenage relationship. While more research needs to be done on this problem, we know that technology and easy access to sexual material is warping young people's views of what is 'normal' or acceptable behaviour.'

A Government spokesman said: 'The number of young people cautioned or convicted for sexual offences has fallen by nearly a quarter over the past five years. However, these young people remain some of the most challenging in society and most have extremely complex issues and needs.

'98% of the 4,562 offenders were boys'

'We are driving up the skills and experience of social workers so they are better able to identify the warning signs much more quickly as well as strengthening guidance on child protection.'

Anyone worried about a child can contact the NSPCC on 0808 800 5000, and children wanting help can call ChildLine on 0800 11 111.

4 March 2013

⇨ The above information is reprinted with kind permission from the Press Association . Please visit www.pressassociation.com for further information.

© Press Association 2013

Neglect: wants and needs

If you're not getting the important things you need, or you're not being looked after properly by your parents or carers you might be experiencing neglect.

Neglect – not being cared for properly

Being looked after properly means that you have access to these things when you need them:

⇨ Clean, warm clothes or shoes

⇨ Comfort and affection

⇨ Enough to eat and drink

⇨ Protection and guidance to keep you away from dangerous situations

⇨ Somewhere warm and comfortable to sleep

⇨ Help when you're ill or you've been hurt

⇨ Support with getting your education.

Being looked after properly also means that you are not left alone for a long time, or have to spend a lot of time looking after other people in your family, without getting any support from an adult.

If any of this is happening to you, you might think that it's your fault. It isn't. Every child and young person has the right to be well looked after, but sometimes parents and

carers are not able to manage this by themselves. If you want to talk about neglect, there are people who care – they will listen to you and help you.

How can I tell people I am being neglected if I'm too embarrassed?

Being neglected can make life difficult for you in lots of ways. It might be that it is hard to keep yourself or your clothes clean, that you are always hungry or tired, or that you never have any money.

You might not want to tell other people if you are worried about what they will think, but it is really important to remember that this is not your fault. There are people who are there to help when young people are neglected. They will have helped other children in similar situations, and they will just want to find ways to make things better for you.

If you are worried about anything to do with neglect, you can always talk to ChildLine – we are here for you no matter how big or small your worry.

Will I get my parents into trouble if I tell someone about being neglected?

There can be lots of different reasons why your parents or carer might be neglecting you. It might be that they are doing their best but just don't have enough money. Maybe they have a problem with alcohol or drugs, or are having problems with their mental health. Whatever the reason, it is still your parents' job to make sure you are properly looked after. There are people who can help your parents with whatever problems they are having, so it is important that they get the help they need.

I'm worried that someone I know is being neglected, but I don't know what to say to them about it?

It's really good that you're looking out for this person. Neglect is quite common (one in ten 11- to 17-year-olds have experienced severe neglect)* so if you're worried about someone, it's a good idea to share how you feel. You shouldn't have to deal with your worries by yourself.

Young people are often more likely to notice when someone their age is being neglected. If you're worried about someone, they might be at risk of neglect if you notice that often:

⇨ They are wearing clothes that don't fit, or are dirty or smelly

⇨ They seem like they haven't washed

⇨ They are hungry or asking for other people's food

⇨ They might often come to school with no lunch

⇨ Their parents don't seem to know where they are or what they are doing

⇨ They don't turn up for school, or arrive late.

⇨ They don't seem to have many friends

⇨ They get sent to school even when they are really unwell.

Maybe you could start by talking to an adult that you trust. You can always call ChildLine on 0800 1111 or contact us online, and tell us what's on your mind if you don't feel comfortable asking your friend about it. You could also look at our page on helping a friend for more ideas on how you could support them.

From: NSPCC (2011) 'Child abuse and neglect in the UK today' London: NSPCC

If I talk to someone, will I be taken into care?

No, speaking to someone about being neglected doesn't mean that you'll automatically be taken into care. The police and social services are there to protect you from being neglected, but they will usually only put you in care if they think it's too dangerous for you to live at home.

There could be lots of different reasons why your parents or carers are finding it difficult to look after you. Social services are there to help your parents work out what's going wrong and get them the support they need to make things better. A first step to your

family getting this help is to talk to someone you trust such as a teacher or a friend's parent and tell them what is happening. If you feel that you don't want to talk to anyone about what's happening or are too scared, you can talk to ChildLine and we can help.

What will happen to my brothers and sisters?

If social services get involved then they will try really hard to find a way of helping your family all stay together if it is safe to do that. Sometimes Social Services will need brothers and sisters to live in different places in order to make sure that each child is looked after properly. They can't promise that you would all stay together but they will always try.

Someone in my family is ill or has a disability. I have to spend a lot of time helping them – does this mean I am neglected?

A young carer is a young person who helps to look after a relative who has a disability or illness (including mental health problems), or a drug or alcohol problem. If you are a young carer, you should still have enough free time to do your school work, see friends or just chill out for a bit.

Social services are there to help you and the person you are caring for, so that you don't end up struggling. If it feels like you are not getting enough support, it is a good idea to ask for some help. You can always talk to ChildLine about anything that is worrying you.

I experienced neglect, things got better for a while, but now they are bad again. What can I do?

If there are positive changes at home (for example, getting support from social services) things will often get better and everyone feels less worried.

Unfortunately, sometimes things might start to get worse again after a while. If this happens to you, it's really important to let people know what is going on. Neglect should never happen, however long it goes on for.

If you think you might be experiencing neglect, it's important to speak to someone who can help. You can always call ChildLine on 0800 1111 or contact us online.

⇨ The above information is reprinted with kind permission from ChildLine. If you are worried about neglect, you can call ChildLine free on 0800 1111 or chat to a counsellor online. Visit www.ChildLine.org.uk for information and support.

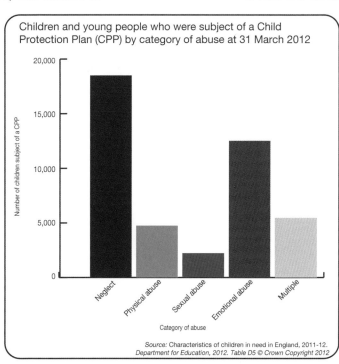

Children and young people who were subject of a Child Protection Plan (CPP) by category of abuse at 31 March 2012

Source: Characteristics of children in need in England, 2011-12. Department for Education, 2012. Table D5 © Crown Copyright 2012

Leanne – 'My experience of neglect'

When Leanne* was at primary school, things at home got so bad that she ran away and put herself in real danger. She tells us how neglect affected her when she was growing up.

Life at home

We led a very chaotic life, moving house all the time. The houses were in bad condition and always dirty. I remember not washing enough, my clothes being dirty, and my hair being messy. At school the kids would call me 'smelly' and 'dirty' and I was bullied all the time. The bullying got so bad that the bullies said that if they saw me out of school they'd kill me. I was really scared that they might.

I was often left to cook my own dinner and do the cleaning. There was no table to eat at. I thought our place was normal until I saw other children's homes which were so very different. My friends at school didn't want to come back to my place.

My mum

I think mum just didn't know how to be a good mum. She had a terrible childhood herself. When I was really small, mum used to tell me she loved me, but as I got older this stopped and I thought she didn't love me anymore. Her moods were up and down, she drank a lot and there were often big rows, sometimes violent, with her partner. I was frightened of her when things got bad.

I always got good grades at school, but after a while I just gave up. I didn't see the point in trying. I think the teachers should have noticed something was wrong, but no-one asked me what was going on. I felt worthless and alone – nothing was working in my life.

Running away

I got to the point where I was really stressed and not sleeping. I felt isolated. There was no-one to turn to, only my mum, and that wasn't working. It all got too much for me, I was utterly miserable, so I ran away from home.

Before I ran away I went to social services, I told them how stressed I was and that I wasn't going home. They gave me some money and told me to stay with a friend for the night but I was worried if I did that my mum would find me.

ChildLine

I was 11 years old and on my own at night and scared. Luckily, I saw the number for ChildLine in a phone box and I spoke to a counsellor who listened to me. They managed to find me a safe place to stay but I was told I was only allowed to stay for a few days. Then I was in care for six months and it didn't work out, so I ended up back at home. Things soon became unbearable, so I ran away again. I slept rough for three nights. After that I was put into another foster home where I stayed for several years.

I can't help but think that it could have been much better for me if our problems had been recognised, and mum and I had got more help earlier. Through all those difficult years ChildLine was there for me. If they hadn't helped me when I ran away I hate to think what could have happened to me. I really don't know what I would have done without ChildLine.

*Name has been changed.

⇨ The above information is reprinted with kind permission from ChildLine. If you are worried about neglect, you can call ChildLine free on 0800 1111 or chat to a counsellor online. Visit www.ChildLine.org.uk for information and support.

Action on neglect

A resource pack from Action for Children.

Views of young people

The young people who formed one of our consultative groups for the Action on Neglect project told us what they thought neglect meant from their own experiences.

What is neglect?

⇨ Not enough love

⇨ Parents and step-parents not spending time with me

⇨ Parents and step-parents having no interest in me

⇨ Not being able to confide in my mum or dad

⇨ Having to look after brothers and sisters – you end up doing your parents' job, the responsibility is passed to you

⇨ Parents have no interest in school and not going to parent's nights; not helping with homework

⇨ Parents have no control

⇨ Parents neglect themselves

⇨ The parents can't care – they may be stressed from moving around a lot

⇨ Messy hair and clothes – you get judged for your appearance

⇨ It's one thing to say they love you but they have to do things to show it

⇨ There are no guidelines for parenting

⇨ Love is a doing word

What does neglect feel like?

⇨ You have to put up a pretence – once in care you feel you are breaking through that barrier, you can be yourself and feel more confident, care makes you come out of your shell

⇨ You cover up your feelings

⇨ It's hard having no friends and other kids don't realise how difficult that is

⇨ Having friends helps but you don't like upsetting your friends when you talk about it so you try not to very much

⇨ You get the mickey taken out of you but you blame yourself, not your parents

⇨ At school, you can't concentrate on the subject because things are bad in your life and then you feel it's unfair because you get told off

⇨ At school a boy shouted at me that I was from a bad family, so then I didn't want people to know. Another girl told everyone and then I got the mickey taken out of me

⇨ Feeling it was too crowded in our house, too chaotic, not enough money and like having two families – my parents in one and me and my brother in the other

⇨ I didn't think about it much at the time, but when I look back I think it shouldn't have happened

This is what the young people in our consultative group would like to say to professionals and adults who want to help them:

Dear Des the Professional,

We know that many of you try to help us but sometimes you can have the opposite effect, so here are our thoughts about how you can best do it. Firstly, don't make assumptions about us, our situation and stories – we are more than what you read in our case files and you can't always believe everything that's in them. You do know some things about us but probably not all, although you sometimes seem to think you do. Our situations can be complex and may be hard for you to understand, so you need to take time to get to know us as individual human beings.

We need to be helped to find the right person to open up to – although most people can learn to relate to us well if they have the right personality. You need to be approachable and have a normal conversation with us; we like you to be professional but not cold. You need to be straightforward with us and not give us cryptic or confusing messages. And if possible, not write things down when you're talking to us.

Sometimes you take what we say the wrong way or act like it's a joke – you need to take us seriously and really LISTEN. Please don't say bad things about our parents to us, even if you think they have been 'bad' parents. But listen to us if we say things against them, because we lived with them and know what it was like. And also don't make us feel that everything's our fault.

We need to have people's jobs explained to us. Who are they? What is their role? Why and how might they help us?

Social workers – there are so many of them! Why can't we just have one?

What we would like is a social worker who cares but doesn't try too hard – social workers sometimes get a bit clingy and over-do it, making us feel stifled. And they can ask too many questions and the kind of things they ask can be difficult to answer. Some are quite intimidating and others are too informal and chatty and it makes us wonder if they are any good and know what they are doing. A good one asks you want you want and tries to help you get it; some asked our parents what they wanted but they didn't ask us.

Social work laws and procedures sometimes make things change for us but they can also create more problems and get in the way of helping us. For example, Looked After Children Reviews are held too often if things are going well in our lives. We don't want to be going through all that intrusion in our lives more often than necessary.

Some of us had family support workers and some of them could have helped our family more. For example, some of us played a game where you pick up a card with an emotion on it and then we had to tell our parents how we felt in certain situations or how they made us feel. Then when the family support worker left we had big family arguments about it. So it's not a good idea to open up feelings and then just leave – everyone shouts at each other and then we're all upset. Some of us had family support for years and years and it didn't really help us much. Please respect our views if we don't want to have this sort of help.

Some parents can change and others can't. Some are given too many chances and we are left too long at home. But when we do have to be moved you need to give us clear explanations about why or we will blame the care service. In some cases parents are just overwhelmed with their problems and we're not sure if anything could have really helped them to look after us better. Although some do not get enough chance to change – it depends on the individual circumstances.

Sometimes some of us run away from home and school: you need to realise that we're trying to tell you something when we do this. Try asking something other than 'are there any problems?' because we'll probably just say no. And if we don't want to talk to our parents about the problems, please don't make us.

'I regret the past but not where the past has brought me to; being in care has changed me in a good way.'

We'd like you to listen and look out for signs of children being in need of attention – like being bullied or showing behaviour that is risky for them.

When we go into care, we often put ourselves down a lot. But if we get a good match, with the right foster carers, it's really good and better than being at home with someone who can't look after us.

The right foster carers are ones who like you and show an interest in you, make an effort, focus on you more and

ask your opinions like what music you want to listen to in the car. Some are better than others and you either get on or you don't – you have to like or even love each other. Some children love being in care because it's made such a difference to them. But we need to realise that it's down to us to change ourselves, mainly.

There are other people who try to help us, like teachers. Some of them could be more understanding about things like why we don't have our PE kit and haven't done our homework – they need to ask us why and not just tell us off. Sometimes teachers are not there for us when we need them but can be there too much when we don't. Then they want to know everything, whereas sometimes we need a bit of space. Teachers need more training in this or we need a support worker at school we can talk to.

We can feel overwhelmed at school and get panic attacks – we need a quiet room or somewhere to de-stress. The medical room can be OK but is usually not very relaxing and in some schools other pupils can see that you're going there and wonder why.

Personal Education Plans (PEPs) can be a good thing for some young people but can be too intrusive if we are doing well and don't really need one. We have to have a PEP because we're in care and people expect that we need one just because of that, when we may be doing fine with our school work. We'd rather not be treated differently to other young people because other people at school then ask us why we are having meetings.

Youth workers can be good – some of them we turn to because they are usually understanding and not patronising. They don't ask too many questions and yet you can tell them things, maybe because you choose to.

You can shut them off easier when they bug you!

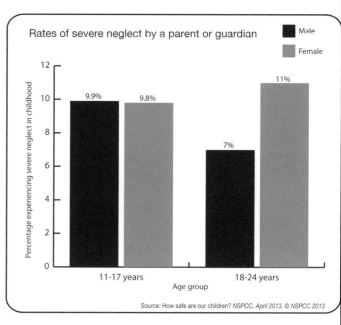

Rates of severe neglect by a parent or guardian

■ Male
■ Female

Percentage experiencing severe neglect in childhood

9.9% 9.8% 7% 11%

11-17 years   18-24 years
Age group

Source: How safe are our children? NSPCC, April 2013. © NSPCC 2013

Some of us have been helped by CAMHS staff whereas some say they were hideous and just asked 'why are you here?' Some of us have been labelled as having Asperger's or autism and this can help (or sometimes not) but it needs to be explained to us properly.

You adults need to recognise the importance of our friends to us; for some of us our friends were the only people we could talk to before we went into care. But we need to choose our own friends. It's hard for some of us to socialise and make new friends – you need to see that we all manage this in different ways and help us with this. Sometimes we feel pushed into making friends.

And it is really good to get to know other kids in care because they know what we're going through.

So please listen to what we have said in this letter and take our advice – it will make it easier for everyone – for us and for you.

Thanks,

The young people

March 2013

⇨ The above information is reprinted with kind permission from Action for Children. Please visit www.actionforchildren.org.uk for further information.

© *Action for Children 2013*

Time to end the neglect of child neglect

Neglect is among the most pervasive forms of child abuse with the power to blight children's lives in the short and long term. It damages their physical, educational and emotional development, as well as their friendships and behaviour.

Yet when it comes to providing effective prevention and protection against these harms, it seems neglect is, itself, too often neglected by professionals.

According to campaigners from the UK charity Action for Children and researchers at the University of Stirling, neglect poses real and continuing challenges for researchers, theoreticians and national and local policy makers. Their assessment of services and procedures across the UK concludes that safeguarding and child protections systems are struggling to provide a swift and effective response.

'All too often children have to endure a chronic lack of physical and emotional care over long periods of time before they receive help. And too often that help is too little, too late,' they warn in the first of a planned annual series of child neglect reviews.

Definition difficulties

As the report recognises, the concept of neglect is difficult to apply. While its florid manifestations – an abandoned, ragged or ill-fed child – may prompt a speedy response, other forms are not so obvious. Neglect is often chronic rather than acute and relies for definition on an accumulation of minor events rather than a single incident.

Neglected children may be ignored emotionally and physically by their parents, lack parental support for

schooling and health care, or be denied opportunities for fun and friendship. Underlying issues may include parental incapacity due to addiction or illness and stresses such as family breakdown or domestic violence. These, in turn, may be exacerbated by societal factors like low income, stigmatisation and overcrowding.

The development of effective services has also been hampered by the lack of any single cause or desired outcome for professionals to focus on. Not only are they unsure of what to do for the best, but getting services can also be cumbersome. Child protection systems intended to help can easily hinder – not least where evidence of a pattern of neglect has to be gathered and then proved in court.

The Action for Children review fairly observes that awareness of neglect issues is improving in the UK, prompted recently by Prof. Eileen Munro's government-ordered review of children's social services in England. Independent reviews on early intervention and poverty commissioned by government from the MPs Graham Allen and Frank Field have further underlined the scope for prevention.

A multi-pronged approach to prevention

But what should policy makers and practitioners be doing to bring children's needs into clearer focus and replace bureaucratic delays with an integrated and early response?

There have been many suggestions about the kind of multi-pronged approach needed to match the complexities involved. Professor Munro called for a shift away from procedures and recording towards greater expertise in supporting families in a non-stigmatising way. Graham Allen highlighted the benefits of regularly assessing the emotional and social development of infants and young children.

The authors of the Action for Children review accept that existing policies and guidance have been developed with good intentions but that 'a distance has developed between common-sense empathy with the unhappiness of hungry, tired, unkempt and distressed children and an overly bureaucratic and anxiety-ridden system for reaching out to help them'.

The report calls for a priority commitment from government to early intervention provision whose effectiveness is judged by outcomes for children rather than service outputs. It also insists that neglected children must have access to long-term personal support services, as well as intensive support for those in greatest need.

Other key areas for improvement are identified as:

⇨ Collecting better and more consistent data about child neglect and the effectiveness of prevention and protection services. UK surveys suggest one in ten children experience at least one problem with parental care and that multiple, regular difficulties affect just under two per cent. However, children's day-to-experiences of neglect are likely to be more complex than simple statistics can demonstrate.

⇨ Creating a truly integrated and responsive system, recognising that the chronic, multifaceted nature of neglect is what makes it so damaging to children's healthy development.

⇨ Raising public awareness and professional knowledge so early signs of neglect can be acted upon. Teachers and others who work with children in 'universal' settings should be trained to understand the benefits of early intervention.

⇨ Offering effective, evidence-based help. Surveys conducted for the review suggested that some families are bombarded with services that apparently make little difference to the quality of children's lives.

Clearly, definitions of child neglect vary widely and discussions can still be too broad and unbridled to produce clear proposals for tackling it. There can be no glib or easy solutions. Nevertheless, this report lays the foundations for the kind of multi-pronged approach that is needed to prevent neglect and protecting children for whom growing up is made miserable.

References

Burgess, C., Daniel, B., Scott, J. et al. (2012). Child Neglect in 2011. London: Action for Children. http://www.actionforchildren.org.uk/neglect.

Allen, G. (2011). Early Intervention: The next steps. London: The Stationery Office.

Munro, E. (2011). The Munro Review of Child Protection: Final report: A child centred system, London: The Stationery Office.

3 December 2012

⇨ The above information is reprinted with kind permission from Prevention Action. Please visit www.preventionaction.org for further information.

© Prevention Action 2013

Why are some children and young people at greater risk of suffering from abuse and neglect?

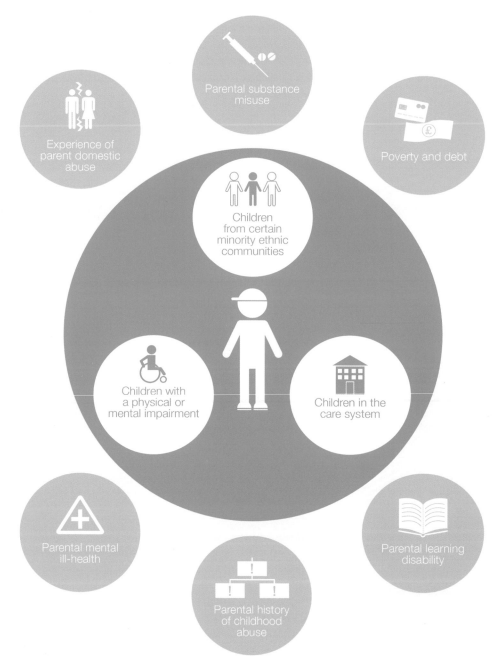

Experience of parent domestic abuse

Parental substance misuse

Poverty and debt

Children from certain minority ethnic communities

Children with a physical or mental impairment

Children in the care system

Parental mental ill-health

Parental history of childhood abuse

Parental learning disability

Source: How safe are our children? NSPCC, April 2013. © NSPCC 2013

Tackling child abuse linked to faith or belief

The belief in witchcraft has in recent years led to some horrific cases of child abuse and child-killing. Justin Bahunga reports on measures to tackle this growing problem.

The belief in supernatural forces, good or evil, that can control people and events is widespread across faith and culture. In many societies, where such beliefs are held, it is believed that those forces can be acquired voluntarily or involuntarily. The belief in witchcraft has sometimes led to harmful behaviours including emotional and physical abuse, infanticide and even sexual abuse.

While accusations of witchcraft have targeted old people in the past, particularly women, there has been a growing trend to accuse children of being witches or possessed by evil spirits, not just in war-torn Democratic Republic of Congo and other poverty-stricken areas of Africa, but also in the UK. Most of the cases reported in the UK have been within black communities. They have included the high profile cases of Victoria Climbie (2000), Child B (2003) and Kristy Bamu (2010).

The diagnosis of witchcraft is not based on any scientific or medical evidence. There is no other method identifying whether a child is 'a witch' apart from the words of faith leaders or other people. There is no method – scientific or otherwise – of proving that a child diagnosed as a witch is responsible for harming people in any way. Once a child is branded by a faith leader, everyone else in the particular community or congregation believes this is the case. For example, some of the cases that Africans Unite Against Child Abuse (AFRUCA) has dealt with have included a child accused of making her step-mother barren and a child with a physical disability accused of demonic possession because of their

physical state such as epilepsy, being left-handed, a hand with an extra finger, skull deformation, etc. In the case of 15-year-old Kristy Bamu, the fact that he had wet his pants was considered enough evidence that he was a witch.

The accusation of witchcraft dehumanises and criminalises the child, thereby opening the door for many forms of abuse including physical abuse, emotional abuse and neglect, while at the same time putting the child at risk of sexual abuse.

Once a child has been branded as a witch or possessed by evil spirit, she/he has to go through a process of deliverance/exorcism. The exorcism rites may include prayer or fasting and when this fails the next stage is to resort to physical force by 'beating the devil out of the child'. Cases of semi-strangulation allegedly to 'squeeze life out of the devil', stabbing to 'create a way out for the evil spirit' have been reported. There also have also been cases of beating, burning or putting pepper or chilli in the eyes of a child.

In extreme cases, identifying a child as a witch is the first episode in a serious of incidents of escalating violence which can lead to death. In cases where children survive, the effects of branding a child as a witch are long-term and devastating and include post-traumatic stress disorder, depression and feeling suicidal.

The two case studies below highlight the kind of abuse that vulnerable children can be subjected to following accusations of witchcraft.

Case Study 1: Child B

Child B (name withheld for her protection) was brought to the UK by her aunt who passed her off as her daughter. The aunt, Child B and two other adults lived in the same flat. An eight-year-old boy who lived with them one day accused Child B of being possessed and the adults agreed that this ten-year old girl was a witch and that she was practising an evil form of witchcraft. She was starved, cut with a knife, hit with a belt and shoes. She had chilli peppers rubbed into her eyes and was repeatedly slapped, kicked and bitten. At one stage, she was put in a laundry bag to be thrown in a river and was told 'this is the day that you are going to die'. She was eventually discovered by a street warden on the steps to the block of her apartment in East London covered in cuts and bruises and with swollen eyes. The police found an entry in the notebook of her aunt which talks about Child B being branded as a witch at a church event.

Case Study 2: Kristy Bamu

Kristy Bamu, a 15-year-old boy came to visit his sister and her boyfriend in London along with his siblings for Christmas in 2010. During their stay the sister's partner, Eric Bikubi, accused all three children of having Kindoki (a word meaning witchcraft in the Democratic Republic of Congo).

However, it was Kristy who became the focus of Bikubi's attention after he found a pair of wet pants belonging to Kristy. Wetting is an act popularly linked to witchcraft. Bikubi then accused Kristy of trying to harm his child. The child suffers from a congenital disease and was in hospital before Kristy and other siblings came to visit Bikubi's family. He punched, kicked and head butted him before beating him with a metal weight-lifting bar as hard as he could and knocking out his teeth with a hammer.

Bikubi also ripped apart one of his ears with a pair of pliers and broke four floor tiles on his head, he also forced Kristy's siblings to join in the violence and help clear the

blood. On Christmas Day, with his face beaten to a barely recognisable pulp, Kristy was thrown into a bath and he drowned because he was too weak to keep his head above the water.

The scale of the problem

The research conducted by Eleanor Stobart in 2006 reported 74 cases of abuse linked to a belief in witchcraft and spirit possession; 38 cases involving 44 children were confirmed as faith-related. Some of the cases involved semi-strangulation allegedly to 'get life out of the devil' and a couple of cases consisted of stabbing of a child to create an outlet for the spirit to get out of the child. AFRUCA deals with around a dozen cases each year.

However, the experiences of both AFRUCA and experts such as Eleanor Stobart suggest that the numbers are higher than those that are reported by the different agencies. There are a number of reasons for this. First, many practitioners are unable to detect faith-based abuse and so the incidents are often recorded under the usual forms of abuse, i.e. physical, emotional, sexual abuse and neglect without ever finding the source of the problem; victims do not report faith-based abuse because they either believe the accusations that are made about them or they fear repercussions if they report the abuse. For example, they could fear that the evil spirit will turn against them or that the community will ostracise them for denouncing a faith leader.

Who is at risk?

Although it may seem that children are identified as 'being possessed' and therefore targets for faith-based abuse randomly, they are most likely to become victims if they are already vulnerable, unprotected or can be identified as outsiders. Children at risk include:

⇨ Children with a disability such as autism, epilepsy, Down's syndrome, dyslexia, etc.

⇨ Albinos.

⇨ Children living away from home in private fostering situations or in domestic servitude situations.

⇨ Children living with a step parent, with one of the natural parents absent or dead.

⇨ Children whose parents have been branded as witches.

⇨ Children who are seen as 'naughty' or who have challenging behaviour.

⇨ Precocious children.

⇨ Left-handed children.

⇨ Children who are living within a polygamous setting.

Key triggers to accusations and fraud

Families in migrant communities are faced with many problems and culture and religion can become important

to them as a coping mechanism. In situations where belief in witchcraft and spirit possession is very prevalent, fraudsters passing off for healers or faith leaders exploit the community's vulnerability by promising miracles to fix their problems. Vulnerable children are falsely accused of being responsible for their communities' misfortunes and branded as witches or possessed by evil spirits, needing deliverance by faith leaders who are paid for the job.

The problems faced by new migrant families include: immigration status; lack of social support system enjoyed back home (child care, family mediation); lack of support for children with severe behaviour problems or with disabilities; people suffering post-traumatic stress disorder; unemployment and underemployment; former child soldiers needing special support; exclusion from school and underperformance; social exclusion creating a sense of powerlessness; child trafficking and exploitation; experience of harassment, racial discrimination leading to withdrawal from seeking appropriate services and low self-esteem; linguistic difficulties leading to lack of understanding of their needs, especially children.

Key issues

Although awareness is increasing about faith-based abuse in the UK, there are still a number of hurdles to overcome. AFRUCA's 11-year experience of working with African Communities has demonstrated that education of the community on child protection is vital. Equally important is the training of practitioners. The key challenges are:

⇨ Limited resources to carry out wide-ranging awareness-raising programmes among the new communities regarding the laws and regulations relating to child protection and safeguarding.

⇨ Limited resources to work with faith organisations to ensure that they comply with child protection guidelines in places of worship.

⇨ Absence of appropriate regulatory and policy action to better protect children accused of being witches.

⇨ Lack of adequate social and economic support for families to alleviate their social plight.

⇨ Lack of a system of registration or monitoring for faith leaders. For example, anyone can establish a church with responsibility for hundreds of people including children without an obligation to have child protection project policies in place.

⇨ Lack of a uniform and systematic recording of abuses linked to accusations of witchcraft and spirit possession by government agencies nation-wide.

Many victims are also vulnerable to child trafficking. Children who are thrown on the street having been accused of witchcraft are vulnerable to trafficking, while others undergo religious rituals before they are taken out of the country of origin to promise that they will not give the identity of traffickers.

Tackling witchcraft-related abuse

The belief in witchcraft is not a problem in itself. However, it becomes a problem when it leads to accusations that trigger acts of persecution, including psychological, emotional and physical abuse and even death.

The vast majority of Churches do a great job for the community but there are rogue faith leaders who tarnish the image of religion by exploiting the most vulnerable for financial gains. African-based churches are growing in the UK and while the overwhelming majority are legitimate and benefit their communities, the lack of regulation means that the rogue churches can develop unchecked.

There is need for appropriate regulatory and policy action to better protect children accused of being witches to supplement actions taking place as outlined in the National Action Plan.

What's the Government doing?

The UK Government has established a National Working Group on Child Abuse linked to Faith or Belief. In August 2012, the Group published a National Action Plan to tackle child abuse linked to faith or belief.

The plan of action sets out four key areas of work:

1. Engaging communities: engaging key stakeholders (parents, community and faith leaders) and listening to the voices of young people.

2. Empowering practitioners: raising their knowledge and skills level to understand the issue and to gain the confidence to detect such abuses and to better protect children at risk of suffering from abuse linked to faith or belief; to promote greater contact between communities and Local Safeguarding Children Boards.

3. Supporting victims of abuse linked to faith or belief and witnesses. This has been a missing point which is partly responsible for underreporting.

4. Communicating key messages: better rapport between communities, practitioners and the media and general public in order to build better understanding of the rights of children as well as having better responses and responsible public discourse when abuse happens.

The Government's decision to establish a National Working Group on Child Abuse linked to faith or belief and drawing an action plan is very welcome. It covers most of the areas that need to be addressed such as engaging the community, training practitioners and supporting victims of abuse. New developments such as supporting witnesses and communicating key messages are welcome developments.

⇨ The above information originally appeared in *Every Child Journal* and is reprinted with kind permission from Africans Unite Against Child Abuse (AFRUCA) UK.

© AFRUCA 2013

A childhood lost

A report on child marriage in the UK and the developing world from the UK All-Party Parliamentary Group on Population, Development and Reproductive Health.

Foreword

When I look at my grandchildren playing together and think of their future, I can be fairly confident that in our family culture my granddaughters will have equal opportunities to my grandsons to achieve whatever they want in their lives.

Ten million girls around the world however are not so fortunate. Every three seconds, a girl is coerced or forced into marriage, losing her childhood, her dreams and the opportunity to make her own choices about her life and relationships.

These girls are expected to marry early, have children and forget about any life except serving those children, their husbands and families – if they survive long enough to do so. It is usually a grim prospect of suffering until they die.

This is not just bad news for the girls themselves, who often have no education as a consequence. It also means that too many children are born into a world that is already overpopulated and half of the productive population of a developing country cannot participate fully in their societies because they are uneducated and unable to contribute to the workforce. Countries where girls are educated, marry later and have fewer children show higher economic growth and a better standard of living for all.

Child marriage is usually forced marriage, although of course some may want to marry the partner of their parents' or their own choice.

We must remember that it happened in our own country not so long ago in many families. The eldest daughter of Queen Victoria, for example, was betrothed at the age of 15 and married at 17.

Girls are tricked into being taken from this country by their families to marry men they have never seen. This report tells the story of some of them. In other countries child and forced marriage is widespread and horrifying in its cruelty in some cases. Our report has put on record the suffering of these girls and has heard from many specialists in the field on the causes in families and society of this practice. We also look for ways of discouraging child marriage in the long term, both by further legislation in this country and by encouraging other countries to follow.

Don't just read the summary and file this away somewhere. Resolve to do something about our sisters worldwide whose cries are not heard.

Baroness Jenny Tonge, Chair of the UK All-Party Parliamentary Group on Population, Development and Reproductive Health.

Executive summary

Child marriage, which is marriage that takes place before one or both of the spouses has reached adulthood, is a global phenomenon. This is despite the fact that it is illegal according to international – and, in most cases, national – laws. Although it is most prevalent in the developing world, there is increasing evidence of child marriage happening in the UK and other developed countries. The number of British children being forced into marriage is hard to gauge, as these marriages are not usually officially registered, but we do know that 14% of calls to the Forced Marriage Unit's helpline during 2012 were regarding the marriage of children under 15 years old (UK Forced Marriage Unit website). The British Government has demonstrated a strong political will to tackle forced marriage in the UK, yet awareness of its extent and its consequences both here and in the developing world is limited.

11 October 2012 saw the first International Day of the Girl. This was an opportunity to recognise the rights and potential of girls worldwide, but also to bring attention to the challenges faced by so many of them, including early marriage. On the day, the United Nations' Population Fund (UNFPA) released new data that predicts that, if child marriage prevalence trends continue, by 2020, 142 million girls will be married before they are adults. This means that, due to a rising global population, child marriage rates are likely to increase to around 14 million girls being married per year (UNFPA, *Marrying Too Young*).

Specific causes and practices vary according to context, yet there are common themes. In some areas, child marriage has been practised for many centuries, while in others it emerges as a response to conditions of crisis including political instability, natural disasters and civil unrest. This report highlights poverty and gender inequality as drivers of child marriage. While boys are married when they are children too, it is girls who are disproportionately affected by child marriage. Many parents marry their daughters off young to 'protect' them from poverty, sexual harassment, the stigma of extramarital sex and sexually transmitted infections, as well as to reduce their own economic burdens. Yet, child marriage in fact entrenches these problems and does little to protect girls or boys.

In the developing world, a lack of access to education is both a symptom and a cause of child marriage, especially for girls, many of whom get very little formal education as they are valued more for their future roles as wives and mothers. Child brides are generally expected to bear children from an early age, leading to a prolonged period of reproduction and larger numbers of children. As a result, they miss out on opportunities to learn, to build financial independence and to make autonomous decisions about their futures – and these effects are passed on to successive generations.

Child marriage is a shocking infringement of human rights and the rights of the child. It has many significant and worrying consequences:

⇨ It leads to higher rates of maternal mortality and morbidities.

⇨ It contributes to infant mortality and poor child development.

⇨ It is associated with violence, rape and sexual abuse.

⇨ It increases population growth and hinders sustainable development.

⇨ It takes away opportunities for education and training, especially for girls and women.

⇨ It is associated with and helps perpetuate harmful traditional practices including female genital mutilation.

⇨ It is a severe threat to combating poverty and the achievement of the Millennium Development Goals.

Khady's story

Khady Koita was married at 13 in Senegal to her 39-year-old cousin, who took her to France, where they had five children. Her marriage was arranged by her grandfather and she explained that, in her community, marriages that keep close links between families are favoured. Marrying dependents off while they are still children prevents them from marrying outside of their village and ethnic group; it is also thought to avert premarital sex.

Even now in 2012 you have some people in Africa who continue to give young girls of 15 years of age to 50-year-olds because for them when the girl gets breasts and you are tall and big, you are ready to marry. They do not think if your mind or if your body is ready. And also they say if you do not marry her now maybe she will get pregnant outside [of marriage]. At that time also it was not like we were all educated. For me my man was not educated. He came from a village and I was educated and I came from the city. And when we came to France he promised my mother I would continue to study but when we came it was another situation. I had five children. Each year I had a child. The violence started in the house because I wanted to study and I wanted to go out and he did not want me to. All the men around said if you let your wife go to study she will get bigheaded and she is not going to listen to you. All the community said your man is your Paradise. (Khady Koita, oral evidence)

Khady explained that, in Senegal, pregnant women have their female relatives to go to for advice and support, yet they typically lack good healthcare and often suffer from maternal morbidities. Giving birth in France, she had access to medical care but no support network around her. Like the other survivors, she felt powerless and isolated after her marriage and this worsened when she became pregnant.

Like the other two survivors who gave oral evidence at the hearing, Khady is aware that child marriage is a cultural, rather than religious practice, yet she pointed out that one of the reasons why girls and boys find it difficult to

fight against their marriages is not only because it will upset their families, but because they are concerned that they are committing a sin.

Khady eventually managed to secure a divorce from her husband, but she had to spend ten years fighting against the French legal authorities, whom she says wanted to uphold the customary law under which her marriage took place. She also had to repeatedly defend herself against her community's accusations that she was betraying their cultural traditions. Now, she is a champion for African women's rights and supports many other women who have suffered violence and abuse, including forced marriage and female genital mutilation (FGM).

Khady described the situation as she has observed it in France:

In France today we have catastrophic problems between us and our children. The parents now know if you marry your child before 18, it is [against] the law and your child is protected and the judge can do things against you, but they are waiting now until after 18. They just try to send the child to Africa for a holiday, and in this holiday they can kidnap them, marry them and keep them in some village far away from the city and they take the passport and the ID, and then they hope she will get pregnant, because if she gets pregnant it is more difficult for her to say no. We have some girls who run away and came back maybe a few years later and some never come back. And now many of them what they do – and it is a tragedy – they accept to go there because they say to me, 'If I don't go there, it is a conflict between me and my parents,' and they accept to go there to make this marriage. (Khady Koita, oral evidence)

November 2012

⇨ The above information is reprinted with kind permission from the UK All-Party Parliamentary Group on Population, Development and Reproductive Health. Please visit www.appg-popdevrh.org.uk for further information.

Sexual abuse

Sexually abused?

What is sexual abuse?

Sexual abuse can include different kinds of activities such as:

⇨ Some types of kissing

⇨ Touching private parts of the body

⇨ Rape (being forced to have sex when you don't want to)

⇨ Being made to look at pornographic videos or magazines

⇨ Other acts which are felt by the child or young person to be abusive.

This is not the kind of sex play which is a normal part of growing up, when children and young people want to find out about each other's bodies, or when people start going out with each other.

Sexual abusers are usually stronger or in a position of power or authority over the child or young person. They use this power to get the person to take part in sexual activities.

The law tries to protect the safety and rights of children and young people. When someone sexually abuses a child or young person they are breaking the law.

Who sexually abuses children?

Abusers are not usually strangers. Most often, they are a relative, friend of the family, neighbour, a lodger, baby-sitter, someone at school, or even a group. Sometimes they can be other young people – a brother or sister or one of their friends. They often secretly abuse more than one child. Sexual abuse is usually carried out by men but sometimes women do it too.

How might someone who has been abused feel?

Being abused leads to feeling which are hard to cope with, such as feeling:

⇨ Dirty

⇨ Depressed

⇨ Ashamed

⇨ Worthless

⇨ Worried about abusing others

⇨ Confused

⇨ Frightened

⇨ Suicidal

⇨ Angry

⇨ Embarrassed

⇨ Anxious

⇨ Worried about sexuality

⇨ Scared about having a boyfriend or girlfriend

⇨ Guilty

⇨ Like running away

⇨ Lonely

⇨ Isolated.

The person carrying out the abuse may be someone who seems to be very nice in lots of ways. This can make it very hard to accept that they are capable of sexual abuse.

Some abusers choose to believe that there is nothing wrong in what they are doing. They can claim that those they abuse encourage them. This can cause people who are being abused a lot of confusing feelings, such as that they are to blame if they didn't tell the abuser not to do it, or if they didn't tell anyone. Many abusers rely on the age, inexperience and fear of people they abuse to be able to carry on with it.

How can abuse affect behaviour?

Sexual abuse can also lead to other problems:

⇨ Not taking care of yourself

⇨ Bad dreams

⇨ Bed-wetting

⇨ Difficulty sleeping

⇨ Running away

⇨ Blanking out the memory

⇨ Losing your temper

⇨ Not being able to make friends

⇨ Self-harming

⇨ Poor concentration

⇨ Using alcohol or drugs

⇨ Eating problems.

People often do their best to cope with painful feelings by trying to forget about them. But this doesn't always work.

Some people feel that the only way to manage what is happening is to run away from home. If this happens, they are in a lot of danger from people who will take advantage of them. It is easy to become involved in crime or prostitution. If you are feeling like this it is VERY IMPORTANT that you get help.

Telling someone else about sexual abuse

There are three important reasons why you should get help:

⇨ Stopping the abuse

⇨ Starting to get over what happened

⇨ Protecting other children and young people.

Telling someone about abuse may be very hard and can feel scary. You may be worried about what will happen if you talk about it, or if anyone will believe you (if they don't, don't give up, try someone else).

Sometimes it can help if you write down what you want to say first. If telling someone you know feels too difficult to begin with, you could try ringing a helpline. They can give you very useful advice about any worries you might have.

You don't have to say who you are if you don't want to, and can say as little or as much as you want.

This may be the first step in helping you think about who else can support you. This could be a:

⇨ Youth worker

⇨ Teacher

⇨ Doctor

⇨ Friend

⇨ Counsellor

⇨ Police officer

⇨ Social worker

⇨ School nurse.

You may find that the person that you decide to talk to will want to report the abuse to a social worker who can take steps to see that it stops. They will usually talk with you about this first.

If you have been abused, or someone else thinks you have been, there will be an investigation. This is when people such as a social worker, doctor or police officer try to find out what has happened, so it can be decided what should be done to help and protect you. If you have been in touch with any other agencies, they may be contacted too.

Some people worry that if they have been in trouble with the police before they will also be punished for being abused, but this is not the case. This can be an upsetting time, but remember there are people who can help you through it.

Whatever happens, even if the abuser is taken to court and is convicted, you are not responsible for what happens.

Getting help with how you feel

Telling someone about abuse will not necessarily take away upsetting feelings. There may be times when it might seem better not to have told anyone.

'Loads of times I thought about taking it back, saying it was all lies. I didn't want to believe it myself. I just wanted my family back to normal. I just thought it would be easier to pretend it hadn't happened.'

For some people it can be very useful to talk to someone trained in understanding how it feels to have been abused, and how to help. This could be a psychotherapist, psychologist, psychiatrist or counsellor. This does not mean you are mad.

You may want to talk about what has happened to you on your own, or in a group with other young people with similar experiences. Sometimes families find it helpful to talk to a professional together. The kind of therapy offered will depend on what is needed – and wanted.

How can therapy help?

Young people who have decided to have some kind of therapy or counselling say that they feel much more positive about life as a result. They feel less depressed and worried, better about themselves and more able to do normal things such as schoolwork.

Who can help?

ChildLine

⇨ Helpline: 0800 1111

⇨ www.ChildLine.org.uk

Children's legal centre (for England and Wales)

⇨ www.childrenslegalcentre.com

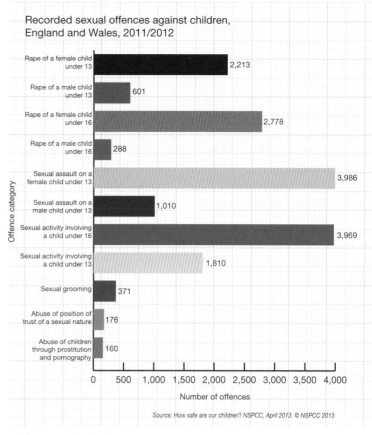

Recorded sexual offences against children, England and Wales, 2011/2012

Offence category	Number of offences
Rape of a female child under 13	2,213
Rape of a male child under 13	601
Rape of a female child under 16	2,778
Rape of a male child under 16	288
Sexual assault on a female child under 13	3,986
Sexual assault on a male child under 13	1,010
Sexual activity involving a child under 16	3,969
Sexual activity involving a child under 13	1,810
Sexual grooming	371
Abuse of position of trust of a sexual nature	176
Abuse of children through prostitution and pornography	160

Source: How safe are our children? NSPCC, April 2013. © NSPCC 2013

NSPCC

⇨ Helpline for children and young people: 0800 1111

⇨ www.nspcc.org.uk

There4Me

⇨ www.achance2talk.com

Youth Access

⇨ 020 8772 9900

⇨ www.youthaccess.org.uk

Get Connected

⇨ 080 808 4994

⇨ www.getconnected.org.uk

Samaritans

⇨ Helpline: 08457 90 90 90 (UK & NI)

⇨ 1850 60 90 90 (Republic of Ireland)

⇨ www.samaritans.org.uk

⇨ The above information is reprinted with kind permission from YoungMinds. Please visit www. youngminds.org.uk for further information.

Thousands of children at risk of sexual abuse claims NSPCC

Thousands of children repeatedly went missing from care homes last year, leaving them at risk of sexual abuse, a leading charity has said.

The NSPCC revealed that 7,885 teenagers and children vanished from care in England and Wales last year, with at least 2,959 going missing more than once, some 35 times.

Around 40% of the youngsters were aged 13 to 17, but some were as young as six.

Tom Rahilly from the charity said: 'The state needs to be a parent for these children. If any other child went missing their parents would move heaven and earth to find them and to understand why they did it. It should be no different for young people in care.

'Repeatedly going missing should be a big warning sign as this kind of behaviour can put them at serious risk of harm such as grooming or sexual exploitation. But we have to understand why they are doing it.

'Children go missing for many reasons - they're being bullied, they've been put in a home miles from their family and they miss them and their friends, or they just don't trust staff enough to tell them where they are.

'Many will have been abused before being placed in care and they need a lot of attention and protection. Going missing for just an hour or two can be long enough for them to come to harm.'

The charity is calling for repeatedly going missing from care to be fully acknowledged as sign that a child is at greater risk of harm.

It also wants care staff to make sure that they listen to children about why they have gone missing rather than simply punishing them, and to work with police to stop children going missing and to return them to safety as quickly as possible.

The NSPCC made a Freedom of Information request to all the police forces in England and Wales to obtain the figures, and 29 out of 43 responded in full.

However the charity said that it is estimated that less than half of all missing cases of this kind are reported to police.

Figures from the Department of Education also differ drastically to those supplied by police, putting the number of missing children at fewer than 1,000, the NSPCC said.

Last month concerns were raised by children's charities about changes to the way that police deal with missing people.

The plans could see the number of cases where officers are called out drop by a third.

Call handlers will class cases as either 'absent', when a person fails to arrive somewhere they are expected, or the more serious as 'missing', where there is a specific reason for concern.

Police deal with around 327,000 reports of missing people each year, the equivalent of around 900 a day, two-thirds of which involve children.

There is often a link between a child frequently going missing and falling prey to sexual abuse.

The NSPCC warned that the changes could put children at risk of being sexually exploited, while the Children's Society claimed that pilots carried out were too short to prove the plans were safe.

A Department for Education spokesman said: 'We welcome the NSPCC's findings. It is simply unacceptable that some residential care homes do not respond immediately when young people go missing. That is why we are taking immediate action to reform the system, so all homes are safe and secure places where vulnerable children can get the support they need.

'We have already changed the rules so that Ofsted can share the names and addresses of care homes with the police to better protect children who go missing. For the first time, we will also begin collecting national data on all children who run away, not just those missing for 24 hours.

'Decisions about whether to place children at a significant distance from their local community will be taken at a much more senior level as a result of a new duty on local authorities.

'Additionally a new regulation will mean children's homes should not be open in areas that are unsafe, and children's home providers will be required to work with the police and LA to consider the risks. We are also taking steps to improve the skills of care home workers so they are better able to identify risks and take action before children run away.'

Chief Constable Pat Geenty from the Association of Chief Police Officers said: 'We know that regularly going missing from home can be a warning sign of child sexual exploitation.

'It can also signify that children and young people may be at risk of other forms of abuse, becoming a victim of crime or involved in criminal activity.

'This is why we have acted to improve our response to risk assessing and responding to missing person cases.'

24 April 2013

⇨ The above information is reprinted with kind permission from the Press Association. Please visit www.pressassociation.com for further information.

© *Press Association 2013*

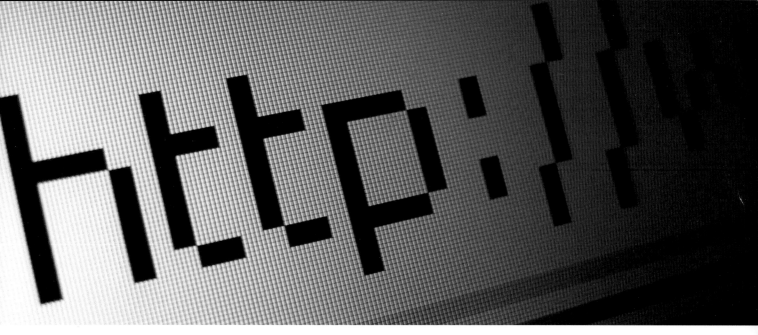

Internet Watch Foundation sexual abuse survey

New study reveals child sexual abuse content ('child pornography') as top online concern and potentially 1.5 million adults have stumbled upon it.

More people in Britain are concerned about websites showing the sexual abuse of children than other types of illegal, illicit or 'harmful' Internet content. However, more than half of people in Britain currently say that they either wouldn't know how to report it if they were to encounter it (40%) or would just ignore it (12%).

The ComRes poll conducted among a representative sample of 2,058 British adults for the Internet Watch Foundation (IWF) shows the vast majority of people in Britain think that child sexual abuse content ('child pornography') (91%) and computer-generated images or cartoons of child sexual abuse (85%) should be removed from the Internet.

⇨ 83% of people overall say they are 'concerned' about child pornography with 74% saying they are 'very concerned'.

Followed by:

⇨ 77% are concerned about computer-generated images or cartoons of child sexual abuse.

⇨ 73% are concerned about terrorist websites.

⇨ 68% are concerned about very extreme/violent pornography.

⇨ 62% are concerned about hate websites (racist or homophobic).

⇨ 61% are concerned about suicide websites.

⇨ 51% are concerned about eating disorder websites.

4% of men – the equivalent of one million men, and 2% of women, the equivalent of 500,000, report actually having come into contact with it, or have stumbled across it.

Four times the proportion of men who acknowledged having come into contact with child sexual abuse content ('child pornography') (4%) say that they would ignore it if they stumbled across it (16%).

The survey also revealed some differences in views between men and women, with women being more concerned than men across all categories of material.

The results come as the IWF reports record times for the removal of online child sexual abuse content from UK public networks. Throughout the whole of 2012, the

IWF logged just 73 UK webpages hosting child sexual abuse images or videos. This compares to 9,477 hosted in other countries around the world.

Of the 73 UK webpages:

⇨ 41 (56%) were then removed within 60 minutes of the IWF notifying the host company or Internet Service Provider (ISP).

⇨ 57 (78%) were removed in two hours or less.

ComRes interviewed 2,058 adults online from 6 to 8 March 2013. Data were weighted to be demographically representative of all British adults aged 18+. ComRes is a member of the British Polling Council and abides by its rules.

Source: A ComRes poll conducted for the Internet Watch Foundation.

March 2013

⇨ The above information is a ComRes poll conducted for the Internet Watch Foundation. Please visit www.comres.co.uk for further details.

Child sexual exploitation

Child sexual exploitation is a form of abuse where young people (under 18) are forced or manipulated into sexual activity.

The abuser may groom the young person into trusting them – this can be done face-to-face or online – and they then exploit this trust for their own gain. Child sexual exploitation can take many forms and victims and perpetrators can be from any social or ethnic background.

Sometimes offenders may get the young person to engage in sexual activity by giving them attention, treats, alcohol, drugs or a place to stay; sometimes they may manipulate the young person into believing they are in a consensual relationship and that they love them. Either way, the young person is being taken advantage of through this controlling behaviour; it is child abuse and the victims face huge risks to their physical, emotional and psychological health. The effects of sexual exploitation on victims can be long-term and last long into adulthood.

Local authorities and the police are committed to preventing child sexual abuse, helping victims and bringing offenders to justice. Communities, however, play a significant part in identifying those who may be at risk and the signs and symptoms involved

What signs are there that a child is being sexually exploited?

Following the Children's Commissioner _Inquiry into Child Sexual Exploitation in Gangs and Groups_, the research and analysis that was conducted identified the following typical vulnerabilities in children prior to abuse:

⇨ Living in a chaotic or dysfunctional household (including parental substance use, domestic violence, parental mental health issues, parental criminality).

⇨ History of abuse (including familial child sexual abuse, risk of forced marriage, risk of honour-based violence, physical and emotional abuse and neglect).

⇨ Recent bereavement or loss.

⇨ Gang association either through relatives, peers or intimate relationships.

⇨ Attending school with young people who are sexually exploited.

⇨ Children with learning disabilities.

⇨ Unsure about their sexual orientation or unable to disclose sexual orientation to their families.

⇨ Friends with young people who are sexually exploited.

⇨ Homelessness.

⇨ Lacking friends from the same age group.

⇨ Living in a gang neighbourhood.

⇨ Living in residential care.

⇨ Living in a hostel, bed and breakfast accommodation or a foyer.

⇨ Low self-esteem or self-confidence.

⇨ Young carers.

The following signs and behaviour are generally seen in children who are already being sexually exploited:

⇨ Missing from home or care.

⇨ Physical injuries.

⇨ Drug or alcohol misuse.

⇨ Regular offending.

⇨ Repeated sexually-transmitted infections, pregnancy and terminations.

⇨ Absence from school.

⇨ Change in physical appearance.

⇨ Evidence of sexual bullying and/or vulnerability through the Internet.

⇨ Estranged from their family.

⇨ Receipt of gifts from unknown sources.

⇨ Recruiting others into exploitative situations.

⇨ Poor mental health.

⇨ Self-harm including thoughts of or attempts at suicide.

How can I get help?

Always call 999 in an emergency, if a crime is in progress or a life is at risk. You can also report incidents and get lots of useful advice from the Child Exploitation & Online Protection Agency (CEOP). For other incidents please contact your local police or alternatively, you can contact ChildLine on 0800 1111.

18 March 2013

⇨ The above information is reprinted with kind permission from the Neighbourhood and Home Watch Network. Please visit www.ourwatch.org.uk for further information.

The grooming of children for sexual exploitation is largely misunderstood

The grooming of children for sexual exploitation is an emotionally dynamic process that is largely misunderstood. Professionals need to start listening to parents as well as children, writes a Pace parent.

Recent investigations on how social services and police 'missed opportunities' to stop the sexual exploitation of teenage girls in Rochdale and Rotherham – not to mention the Jimmy Savile scandal – has ensured child abuse stays firmly in the headlines. There has been a flurry of concern, as professionals produce endless reports on 'system failures'. It now seems that children who report being sexually exploited should be believed after all, not just dismissed as troublemakers. Suddenly, professionals are waking up to the nature of grooming under-age children, and how they are prepared for a life of sexual assault, rape and the enforced selling of sexual services to adult males. However, all of this misses out a vital piece of the jigsaw – the role of parents. What kind of parent would let their child of 14 be out on the streets at night? Aren't they partly to blame?

As a parent of a child who was sexually exploited, I have an obvious interest how professionals respond to allegations of grooming and sexual exploitation. Over the last five years, our family has been one of 600 families supported by Pace, the only UK charity which works alongside the parents of sexually exploited children. Far from being 'dysfunctional' or 'neglectful' parents, the single common denominator that binds us is our fierce, all-conquering love for our children. We did not 'fail to set boundaries' and we did not 'let our children run wild'. Many of us went to desperate lengths to protect our children from their exploiters: some of us emigrated, some left our jobs to keep our children under lock and key; some of us even agreed to have our children put in care – anything to break the vicious cycle of abuse they were trapped in.

Blaming the parent betrays a real lack of understanding of what the grooming process actually consists of. Professionals might be beginning to understand the behavioural signs of grooming – secrecy, multiple mobile phones or sim cards, dressing as an older teenager, disappearances from home or school. Meanwhile the parents themselves are on the receiving end of this at home, desperately trying to make sense of why their 12-, 13-, or 14-year-old daughter has suddenly become aggressive, foul-mouthed and uncontrollable.

What is missing here is an understanding of the emotional dynamics of grooming. For grooming to work, the child needs to be trapped into a coercive relationship with their abuser, and then forced to perform sex with growing numbers of older men. But why don't they just run away? Why do they keep going back for more abuse? Because the grooming has driven a massive wedge between child and parent. The child is convinced that her parents are useless, don't understand her, won't let her have any fun. The predator is now her 'boyfriend' and first real adult lover. The parents' care is now seen as abuse, while the predator's abuse is seen as care and love.

Professionals then try to work with this issue in a child-focused way, just as they have been trained to do. Listen to the child. Look for evidence of problems in the family. Look for difficulties in the parent-child relationship.

Child-centred practice builds on and deepens the rift between parents and child. Parents are seen as unreasonable and therefore need to be kept out of safeguarding meetings. The professionals support the child against the parent, but all the while, the sexual exploitation continues. The professionals are just as powerless to stop the abuse as the parents, but now justify their inaction with the language of children's rights.

Hence the bizarre language of labelling under-age abused children as 'child prostitutes', when the child's consent to sex is actually illegal. Hence the support for the child, once they turn 16, 'choosing' to live with their abuser, in a mockery of equal adult relationships. Even more concerning is the practical advice to children to 'get a contraceptive implant', ultimately for the sole benefit of the queues of adult males who are waiting to have sex with them.

The child's wishes are taken at face value in child protection meetings, when they have completely lost any ability to keep themselves safe. On the other hand, the parents, while now mistrusting of the authorities, still want what is best for their child, but are kept outside of the decision-making process. Because of the emotional effects of the grooming, the child loses the capacity to accept care and protection from their parents, now seen as their enemy. Professionals therefore do a disservice, both to child and parents, in taking the child's wishes for independence at face value, when this continues and deepens their sexual exploitation. Listening to the child may be a hallmark of good practice, but not when the exploited child is simply the mouthpiece of the abuser.

21 January 2013

⇨ The above information is reprinted with kind permission from Parents against child sexual exploitation (Pace).

Protect my future: why child protection matters in the post-2015 development agenda

The widespread failure to protect children is a global crisis, with 0.5-1.5 billion children experiencing violence each year[1], 150 million girls and 73 million boys who are raped or subject to sexual violence[2], and 115 million children engaged in extremely harmful forms of work[3]. This global crisis represents a major violation of children's rights; an unacceptable situation, which must be remedied urgently, no matter what the costs. In addition to impacting on the current well-being of children, the widespread inadequate care and protection of children is also affecting the achievement of broader development objectives relating to child survival and health, education, economic growth and equity. Many girls and boys die each year because they are abused, neglected or exploited. Vulnerable children that survive into adulthood can be at a significant disadvantage, with many experiencing developmental delays, gaps in their schooling and mental and physical health problems due to their maltreatment. The stigma, discrimination and diminished life chances faced by children who are abused, exploited and neglected exacerbates inequity. Whilst the resilience of such children can carry with it some advantage for societies, in general these boys and girls are not able to contribute to economies to their full potential. In addition to

the damaging impacts on children themselves, the negative effects of child maltreatment on human capital, combined with the costs associated with responding to abuse and neglect, means that inadequate care and protection also hinders economic growth.

The alarming impacts of child protection failures are likely to grow in significance unless something is done urgently. Global trends such as climate change, migration and urbanisation are all increasing children's vulnerability and governments are not investing enough resources in building and maintaining comprehensive child protection systems. Children around the world want more support to enable them to grow up free from violence, and within caring, safe families. It is therefore essential that governments, UN agencies and other actors engaged in the design of the framework that will replace the current Millennium Development Goals in 2015:

1. Include a goal on child protection. For example: *All children live a life free from all forms of violence, are protected in conflicts and disasters, and thrive in a safe family environment.*

2. Listen to the voices of children, including vulnerable and commonly excluded groups such as those without adequate care and protection, in debates around the design of the post-2015 development framework and in the implementation and monitoring of this framework.

3. Promote the equitable achievement of all other goals included in the post-2015 development framework through assessing progress within commonly excluded and discriminated against groups, including children without adequate care and protection.

As the quote below indicates, child protection is essential for ensuring strong, flourishing societies; it is the foundation of child well-being that allows girls and boys to thrive, develop and contribute to their full potential.

'You are rebuilding the schools and the roads and the bridges, but you are not rebuilding us and we suffered too much. What is done in Liberia is like constructing a house without cement. It can't hold for too long.' (A young woman in Liberia who as a child witnessed her father and brother being killed and is engaged in commercial sex work, cited in Plan and FHI 2009 p.54)

We must therefore all strive for a world where children can grow up safely in their families, and be free from violence, abuse, neglect and exploitation as this world will be a better place. If we achieve the goal outlined above, alongside targets in areas such as child abuse, early marriage, child labour, and avoiding unnecessary separation from families:

⇨ Girls will not be forced into harmful early marriage, and will be able to wait until they are at least 18 before getting married. This, combined with reduced sexual abuse, will in turn reduce maternal and infant mortality

1 Pinheiro, P (2006) World Report on Violence Against Children. United Nations, New York

2 WHO (2000) World Report on Violence and Health, World Health Organisation, Geneva

3 ILO (2010) Accelerating Action Against Child Labour International Labour Organisation, Geneva

as fewer girls will get pregnant before their bodies are ready.

⇨ Child mortality will fall because children are loved and nurtured within families and girls are not neglected in favour of their brothers.

⇨ Children will not have to work long hours and/or in harmful or hazardous conditions, risking their well-being and health and depriving them of their education.

⇨ Children will be able to learn in schools as they are not terrified of the threat of bullying or corporal punishment or too afraid to go to school because they might be raped by their teachers.

⇨ Human capital potential will not be diminished by children who have experienced so much neglect or abuse that it damages their

physical and mental development and employment prospects.

⇨ The state will be able to re-invest some of the resources it currently spends on supporting victims of abuse.

⇨ Societies will become more equitable as children's chances in life are not seriously damaged by their lack of care and protection. Children's rights to be free from inadequate care and protection will also be achieved.

⇨ Children will grow up in resilient communities that can withstand the shocks of disasters and conflict, and protect them from violence, exploitation, abuse and neglect, even in emergency situations.

⇨ Girls and boys will be happier, safer and more able to develop

to their full potential because they grow up in caring and protective families and get the love and attention that it is human nature to crave.

April 2013

⇨ This paper is part of an inter-agency series on the links between child protection and major development goals produced by Family for Every Child on behalf of Better Care Network, ChildFund Alliance, Consortium for Street Children, Family for Every Child, Keeping Children Safe, Plan International, Save the Children, SOS Children's Villages, Terre des Hommes International Federation and World Vision. Visit www.familyforeverychild.org for more.

The barriers to reporting child abuse

YouGov research for the NSPCC reveals that fewer than one in five UK adults (17%) would report their suspicions of child sexual abuse straight away, even if they had significant doubts.

By Andrew Farmer

A majority of people (58%) are not confident they could spot the signs of sexual abuse in a child they knew, while less than a third (31%) are confident they could spot if the abuse was taking place. Fewer than one in ten people (9%) have had concerns that a child they knew was being sexually abused with 85% of people saying they have not. Of those who have had concerns, more than two thirds (69%) took action while three in ten (30%) either didn't take action, or haven't but still intend to.

The survey found that a plurality of people (28%) would be most likely to report sexual abuse concerns about a child they knew if they had enough evidence to be very sure that it was taking place. More than one in five (21%) would report suspicions if they thought a child was probably being abused, 19% would report if they had a few concerns that a child was being sexually abused and 8%

would be most likely to report when they were completely certain that abuse was taking place.

Reporting fears

The majority (59%) of people said they might be stopped from reporting suspicions of abuse because of fears they were wrong. Almost four in ten (39%) would be worried it might make it worse for the child, one in six (17%) have concerns they would split up the child's family while the same number (17%) worry about the repercussions for the accused. 15% might be put off reporting suspicions over fears about repercussions for them personally and the same proportion (15%) might hold off because they are unsure what happens next.

What should be done

In a separate survey, YouGov also asked on behalf of NSPCC what important things can be done to tackle child abuse in general, in

light of recent media reports around the issue. Almost three quarters (74%) say that children should be encouraged to speak out if they are being abused, two thirds (67%) want tougher sentences for sex offenders and more than six in ten (63%) say promoting ways people can get help when they're worried about a child is important. 59% want more support for the victims and the same number (59%) think it's important to encourage adults to take more responsibility for reporting suspected abuse.

22 May 2012

⇨ The above information is reprinted with kind permission from YouGov. Please visit www.yougov.co.uk for further information.

Victorian child neglect laws in 'urgent' need of overhaul, warns Baroness Butler-Sloss

The current laws on child neglect are not fit for the 21st century and in 'urgent' need of reform, Britain's most senior authority on family law warns today.

By John Bingham, social affairs editor

Baroness Butler-Sloss, the former President of the Family Division of the High Court, is leading a drive to overhaul the current laws, which date back to Victorian times, completely replacing the notion of neglect with a new crime of 'child maltreatment'.

For the first time, inflicting emotional and psychological harm on children would be treated as seriously as causing physical injuries or abandoning them.

It follows a string of cases in which the authorities have failed to step in early enough despite warning signs of neglect and abuse, including the Baby P case and the Edlington torture scandal.

Baroness Butler-Sloss, now a cross-bench peer, has helped draft an amendment to the Government's Crime and Courts Bill, which is currently being considered by a committee of MPs, to overhaul the neglect laws, with the support of the charity Acton for Children.

The current law on 'wilful neglect' is governed by the Children and Young Persons Act 1933.

But it was first laid down in legislation as early as 1868, when the poor law was amended to take account of a cult called the 'Peculiar People' who believed that it was interfering with God's will to give sick children medical assistance.

To secure a neglect conviction the prosecution currently must prove that an adult responsible for a child deliberately assaulted, abandoned or exposed them to suffering or injury to their health.

The new offence would make clear that it is also a crime to do anything which deliberately harmed a child's 'physical, intellectual, emotional, social or behavioural development'.

'The current law explicitly fails to recognise the full range of harm done to neglected children, and creates problems of practice and interpretation for legal professionals,' said the Baroness.

'This cannot be our best effort as law makers at protecting neglected children, and so I am determined to see through a reform of the law in this area.

'I invite my fellow parliamentarians to support this as a matter of great importance and urgency.'

The amendment, which will be considered by MPs today, was published as Action for Children released new research showing that nine out of ten teachers, police officers and social workers regularly come into contact with children they suspect are suffering from neglect – yet as many as 40 per cent feel powerless to intervene.

The report found that 14 per cent of professionals have reported a rise in suspected child neglect over the past year.

Dame Clare Tickell, chief executive of Action for Children, said: 'For the most serious cases we need a law that is fit for purpose and that will give vulnerable children all the protection they need.

'The solutions to child neglect in the UK are manifold, but this is one straightforward and crucial step in the journey.'

Meanwhile a report by Her Majesty's Inspectorate of Probation concluded that schools and social services are routinely ignoring warning signs involving sexual behaviour of children who later go on to abuse other youngsters.

7 February 2013

⇨ The above information is reprinted with kind permission from *The Daily Telegraph*. Please visit www.telegraph.co.uk for further information.

EXISTING LAW

A brief history of child protection legislation in the UK

1889

The Prevention of Cruelty to, and Protection of, Children Act 1889 was the first statute of many to impose criminal penalties to deter mistreatment of children.

1904

Prevention of Cruelty to Children Act 1904 enabled NSPCC Inspectors to remove children from abusive or neglectful family homes.

1908

Punishment of Incest Act 1908 – made sexual abuse within families a matter for state jurisdiction rather than intervention by the clergy.

1926

Adoption of Children Act 1926 – provided adoption for the first time as an alternative to guardianship or institutional care in orphanages.

1948

The Children Act 1948 followed the death in 1945 of a 13-year-old boy, Dennis O'Neill, as a consequence of the neglect and beatings of his foster father. Focused on children in the care of the state and living apart from their families. Established a children's committee and a children's officer to take responsibility for looked after children in each local authority.

1970

The Local Authority Social Services Act 1970 legislated for social services departments, bringing together councils' social work services and care provisions for children, disabled adults and older people.

1978

The Protection of Children Act 1978 legislated against child pornography.

1989

The Children Act 1989 for England and Wales is the most comprehensive piece of legislation concerning children which had ever passed through Parliament. It was far reaching, and sought to provide to clarify the many different pieces of legislation which came before it. It gave children the right to be protected from abuse and defined key elements of the child protection system – including serious harm, the paramountcy principle and parental responsibility.

1991

The United Kingdom ratifies the UNCRC (Convention on the Rights of a Child). This enshrines the basic human rights of all children in the law.

1993

The murder of James Bulger and the subsequent media coverage and trial of his killers caused debate and promoted reform of the juvenile criminal justice system.

1997

The Sex Offenders Act 1997 (UK wide) created the sex offenders register through a series of monitoring and reporting requirements.

1999

The Protection of Children Act 1999 required childcare organisations to inform the Secretary of State for Health about anyone known to them who was unsuitable to work with children.

2000

Eight-year-old Sarah Payne was murdered by convicted sex offender Roy Whiting. Her death led to calls for 'Sarah's Law' to be introduced, similar to Megan's Law in the United States, which allows members of the public to access data relating to sex offenders living in their area.

2001

Cafcass (Children and Family Court Advisory and Support Service) is set up in England and Wales to safeguard and promote the welfare of children involved in family court proceedings.

2003

The Sexual Offences Act 2003 was introduced to update the legislation relating to offences against children. It includes the offences of grooming, abuse of position of trust, trafficking, and covers offences committed by UK citizens whilst abroad. Similar offences were introduced into other parts of the UK by the Sexual Offences (Scotland) Act 2009 and the Sexual Offences (NI) Order 2008.

2006

The Child Exploitation and Online Protection Centre (CEOP) is formed. CEOP works to tackle online child abuse across the UK.

2008

The Home Office launches the Child Sex Offender Disclosure scheme in England and Wales, which would allow members of the public to request information about a named individual to ascertain if they posed a threat to children.

2010

ACPO Child Protection and Abuse Investigation (CPAI) produced a comprehensive Child Protection Delivery Plan (CPDP) in 2010 that cut across the entire range of child protection issues, not just those traditionally related to child abuse investigation. The plan examined areas where practice was in need of development and made 35 recommendations at a national, regional and local level to make a tangible difference to this area of policing. The recommendations have been completed and a new CPDP is under construction and will be released later in 2013. ACPO has also developed an action plan in regards to child sexual exploitation to enhance and support work already ongoing within forces and nationally. That plan covers seven key areas for progress which it expects to report on at the end of July 2013.

Source: Giving Victims a Voice – Joint report into the sexual allegations made against Jimmy Savile. January 2013. NSPCC and the Metropolitan Police Service.

'Historic' abuse?

A guest posting from Tom Perry, for Voice for Children.

I am writing to Voice for Children as someone who in 2001 filed a police complaint about the sexual abuse I experienced as a child. The case was stayed in 2003 using a pretrial 'abuse of process' hearing grounded on the Selwyn Bell precedent which was established just a few months earlier. It says – 'as a result of the passage of time the defendant cannot receive a fair trial'. This meant that the man I accused of abusing me did not have to answer the question in court, and no stayed criminal case has ever returned to court. Following the ruling I approached an independent television production company and four years later the BAFTA award-winning documentary *Chosen* was broadcast.

When in adulthood I finally managed to face the abuse I'd experienced as a child, even I referred to it as 'historic abuse'. The police did the same and media reports on similar cases were and continue to be peppered with the adjective and just look at the Voice blog and others that do such sterling work on the Jersey child abuse cover up, all of them describe child abuse complaints made in adulthood as 'historic'.

People wishing to see truth and justice for abusees should cease using this offensive description. Why?

It is prejudicial and serves to discount, denigrate and dismiss the crimes that abusees have experienced. 'Oh that was all in the past, things are different now.' In reality little in safeguarding has changed since the '50s. There is still no mandatory requirement in England, Wales or Scotland to report allegations of child abuse or actual rape to the police or social services. Just in case you don't believe it: http://www.nspcc.org.uk/inform/research/questions/child_protection_legislation_in_the_uk_pdf_wdf48953.pdf – see page 3 or search key word 'mandatory'.

Regrettably, the appalling description 'historic abuse' entered the lexicon sometime ago unnoticed and to the detriment of complainants. It needs to cease. The mainstream media on Jersey are addicted to this offensive description and here is just one example from the BBC with their latest effort. In England the recent conviction of Father Nick White for child abuse when he was teaching at Downside was reported by all parts of the media in the default 'historic' format despite the abuse on which the trial was predicated occurring only 19 years ago. 19 years!

Would Mrs Doreen Lawrence consider her son Stephen's murder 19 years ago 'historic?' For her, just like me and other abusees who have not had the benefit of having their cases heard in court, it is all too current. Yet the media do not use the 'historic' word to describe Stephen's murder. Why not? Take a few other serious crimes such as aggravated burglary, grievous bodily harm, drug smuggling, or assault, and all are free of the dismissive adjective 'historic'. I have also never seen the crime of rape described as historic. So what is it about child abuse?

For authorities, care homes, schools, young offenders institutes that knowingly and unknowingly employed pederasts to work with children and then concealed discovered crimes, the use of the adjective 'historic' helps dismiss, discount, and consign to history a scandal they wish no one had noticed and which the employer does not wish to address. The same authorities delight in this self-harming description being consistently applied to crime they wish would vanish, but which remain all too current for all Jersey's abusees.

It's child abuse.

16 January 2012

⇨ Article reprinted with kind permission from Voice for Children and Tom Perry. voiceforchildren.blogspot.co.uk.

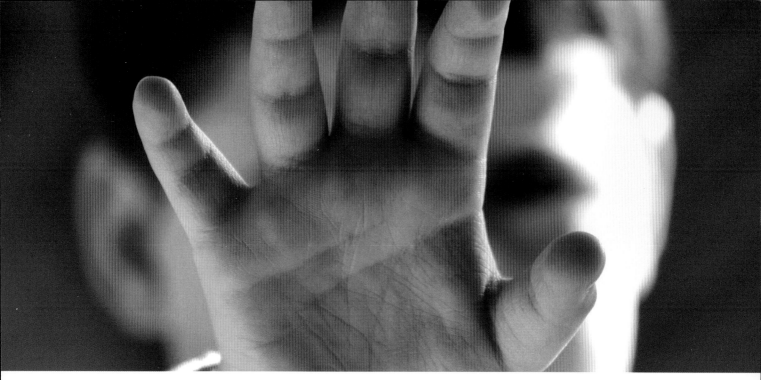

UK 'should follow Ireland by making it mandatory to report child abuse'

Republic of Ireland is to hold referendum on enshrining rights of children in constitution.

By Henry McDonald, Ireland correspondent

The UK should follow the Republic of Ireland by preparing to make the reporting of alleged child abuse mandatory in law, according to the Dublin-based Children's Rights Alliance.

Ireland is holding a referendum on Saturday that aims to enshrine the rights of children in the country's constitution.

Since the 1990s, Ireland has undergone a painful catharsis regarding widespread child sexual and physical abuse in what were once revered institutions of church and state. The republic has published 14 high-powered and damaging reports into the abuse and exploitation of children in church-run orphanages, industrial schools and parishes.

Tanya Ward, the chief executive of the Children's Rights Alliance, whose offices are just a few hundred yards away from the gates of the Irish Parliament, said the UK could learn a lot from the Irish experience of dealing with a legacy of systematic child abuse.

Referring to the 14 separate reports into Irish child abuse scandals, Ward said: 'If there is a common theme running through these reports ... it is that institutions put their own interests before those of children. Certainly the situation we had to deal with in Ireland in terms of the institutional abuse that went on in places like the industrial schools and orphanages is uncannily similar to what is currently emerging [in the UK].'

She said the 1937 Irish constitution had to be amended because it placed more emphasis on the privacy and authority of the family than on the rights of children. In some cases, Ward said, this led to social workers and others in authority in Ireland being put off investigating child abuse within families.

Ward cited forthcoming legislation on the back of the constitutional amendment, should it pass on Saturday, dealing with reporting of child abuse as a lesson for the UK.

'If the people vote yes on Saturday children's rights will be enshrined in the constitution and that will be an important milestone for us because following it there will be legislation which will make it mandatory to report any complaint from any child about abuse. For people working with children they will now be obliged in law to report any concerns those children express to them. If they receive a credible report that a child or young person has been abused they must now under law pass that on to the gardaí and other relevant authorities. This type of law would make a difference in the UK too,' Ward added.

9 November 2012

⇨ The above information is reprinted with kind permission from *The Guardian*. Please visit www.guardian.co.uk for further information.

Charities call for 'mandatory reporting' in the UK

Lead by the National Association for People Abused in Childhood (NAPAC), a coalition of charities is calling for the Government to introduce 'mandatory reporting' in the UK. Under current legislation, reporting child abuse is purely discretionary. This means that if a teacher were to witness their colleague sexually abusing a young pupil they would be under no legal obligation to report the crime to their head teacher, Local Authority Designated Officer (LADO) or the police. The crime could quite easily be swept under the carpet and if the teacher did go ahead and report the abuse, they would have no statutory protection.

Pete Saunders, Chief Executive of NAPAC said: 'Mandatory reporting is long overdue in this country. Parents will probably be shocked to learn that such legislation does not already exist. Staff who suspect abuse may report it, but face no sanction for failing to report. In places such as Hillside First School, Downside, St Benedict's, Stony Dean School and Little Teds Nursery, abuse went unreported to the authorities, leaving children at risk of further abuse.'

Described by school management as a 'lamentable failure', the case at Hillside First School is a stomach-churning example of the kind of scenario in which mandatory reporting was desperately needed: Mr Nigel Leat was jailed indefinitely for abusing children between 2006 and 2010, when he was a teacher at Hillside First School in Weston-super-Mare. A serious case review, commissioned by North Somerset Safeguarding Children Board, revealed that incidents such as inappropriate touching were listed in the school management report. The review also heard that colleagues had, on numerous occasions, advised Mr. Leat that his behaviour was unprofessional. From a total of 30 recorded incidents only 11 were formally reported within the school. At his trial, the Judge described Leat as a 'paedophile of the most sickening order'. He was charged with one count of attempted rape, 22 counts of sexually assaulting a child under 13 and eight counts of sexual assault by penetration. Of his five victims, some were as young as six years old and police found over 30,000 indecent images of children in Leat's possession.

The Mandate Now Coalition launched a petition on 1st May 2013 which urges the Government to introduce the mandatory reporting of known or suspected abuse in 'Regulated Activities'.1 Countries which currently operate mandatory reporting include Australia, Canada, Denmark, Finland, the Republic of Ireland, Spain, Sweden and the USA.

The Mandate Now Coalition includes:

NAPAC – national charity supporting adults who have been abused in any way as children. www.napac.org.uk.

Survivors Trust – national umbrella agency for over 130 specialist rape, sexual violence and childhood sexual abuse support organisations throughout the UK and Ireland. www.thesurvivorstrust.org.

Survivors UK – helps men who have been sexually violated and raises awareness of their needs. www.survivorsuk.org.

Respond – works with children and adults with learning disabilities who have experienced abuse or trauma. www.respond.org.uk.

Innocence In Danger – International Charity recently arrived in the UK which is dedicated to the eradication of child abuse and sex trafficking. www.innocenceendanger.org/en/.

You can sign the Mandate Now petition at: http://www.change.org/en-GB/petitions/educationgovuk-introduce-law-requiring-adults-working-with-children-to-report-alleged-abuse-mandatenow.

4 August 2013

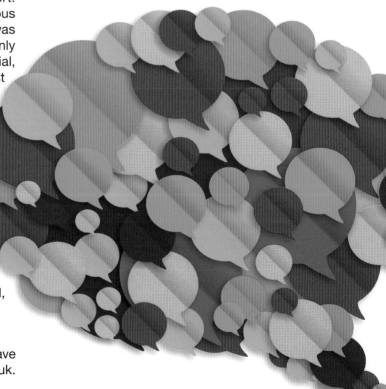

Support for sexual abuse victims in court

Very vulnerable witnesses in sexual exploitation cases should be allowed to give evidence in new specialist courts in the wake of the Rochdale and Jimmy Savile scandals.

Two women MPs, from opposing parties, have joined forces to press for improved support for vulnerable and child witnesses, who often have to endure aggressive cross-examination and questioning from multiple lawyers in intimidating court settings.

The huge volume of unreported allegations against Jimmy Savile demonstrated the importance of better support for witnesses to give victims the courage to come forward.

The recent suicide of the musician Frances Andrade is a stark reminder of just how vulnerable some victims who give evidence against abusers in court can be.

'I have seen first-hand the agony of a fragile young witness doing her best keep it together enough to describe the violent sexual abuse she was subjected to for most of her childhood'

In response, Nicola Blackwood, the Conservative MP for Oxford West and Abingdon and Ann Coffey, the Labour MP for Stockport, have tabled two amendments in support of vulnerable witnesses to the Crime and Courts Bill.

They are calling for new specialist courts for very vulnerable witnesses modelled on specialist domestic violence courts.

In addition they want each child victim to be provided with the support of a Registered Intermediary who would look after them throughout the court process and facilitate two-way communication between the witness and the other participants in the criminal justice process.

NSPCC figures show that only two per cent of young witnesses receive support from Registered Intermediaries, who advise on how best to meet the needs of vulnerable witnesses and ensure that questioning and cross-examination practice maximises the quality of victim evidence.

The amendment also stresses that cases involving very vulnerable witnesses should only be heard by specially trained judges. Each witness should also be assigned a specific court usher, who has taken part in appropriate training, for the duration of their time in court.

If the witness is a victim of sexual abuse they should also be offered an Independent Sexual Violence Advisor to support them throughout the court process.

Ms Blackwood is a member of the Home Affairs Select Committee which is currently conducting an inquiry into child sexual exploitation, and Ms Coffey, the chair of the All Party Parliamentary Group for Runaway and Missing Children and Adults. They recently co-sponsored a Commons debate on sexual exploitation.

Ms Blackwood, said: 'While evidence has to be properly tested in court, I have seen first-hand the agony of a fragile young witness doing her best to keep it together enough to describe, to a roomful of men in wigs, the violent sexual abuse she was subjected to for most of her childhood. All too often, what follows next is aggressive cross-examination to cast the witness as a liar, a prostitute, promiscuous, asking for it, or responsible for her own abuse.

'It doesn't have to be like that. Specialist courts can offer wrap-around support for witnesses while still delivering fairness to defendants. If the court process is less traumatising more victims will come forward, fewer investigations will collapse and more prosecutions will be successful.'

Ms Coffey said: 'Justice is served by making sure that the best quality of evidence is heard in court. Vulnerable children who have to relive horrendous experiences of sexual abuse should get a Registered Intermediary to help them as a matter of course. Current guidance assumes that only very young children or those with a specific learning disability should receive such support.

Failure to provide sufficient support to young witnesses makes them vulnerable to suffering further trauma. Registered intermediaries give young witnesses support in order to ensure that they are adequately prepared for court and protected from further harm. Delay, aggressive cross-examination and the anxiety of seeing their abusers may have lasting effects on vulnerable witnesses and can affect the quality of the evidence that they give.'

27 March 2013

⇨ The above information is reprinted with kind permission from Nicola Blackwood, MP for Oxford West and Abingdon. Please visit www. nicolablackwood.com

Key facts

- ChildLine received almost 50,000 cries for help from children and young people in the 12 days from Christmas Eve 2011 to 4 January 2012. Family problems remained the primary concern of children and young people who contacted ChildLine, accounting for 14 per cent of the total counselling interactions. (page 2)

- In March 2012 59,000 boys and 50,900 girls aged 10 – 15-years-old were classified as being 'in need' in England. (page 4)

- An NSPCC report released in 2011 revealed that nearly a quarter of young adults (24.1%) experienced sexual abuse by an adult or by a peer during childhood. (page 5)

- Almost one in ten children aged 11-17 have experienced sexual abuse in the past year (2011). Teenage girls aged between 15 and 17 years reported the highest past year rates of sexual abuse. (page 5)

- In October 2010 more than 1,000 teachers were sacked in Kenya for sexually abusing girls; most of the victims were aged between 12 and 15. (page 6)

- In 2008 ChildLine reported that 96% of children calling ChildLine because they were being sexually abused knew their abuser. (page 6)

- In 2010 the NSPCC reported that one in four offenders convicted of child Internet porn held positions of trust including teachers, clergy and medical professionals. (page 6)

- Nearly 65% of children calling ChildLine in 1986 said the sexual abuse had been going on for more than a year but by 2006 that had dropped to 23%. (page 7)

- As many as one in four 11- and 12-year-olds experience something on a social networking site that bothers them almost every day. (page 7)

- There were more than 21,500 recorded sexual offences against children in the UK in 2012 alone, including almost 6,000 rapes. (page 12)

- A quarter of nine- to 16-year-olds have seen sexual images online in the last year. (page 12)

- The NSPCC found there were more than 5,000 cases of abuse by under-18s reported to the police between 2010 and 2013. (page 13)

- In 2006 research revealed 74 cases of abuse linked to a belief in witchcraft and spirit possession; 38 cases involving 44 children were confirmed as faith-related. Some of the cases involved semi-strangulation allegedly to 'get life out of the devil' and a couple of cases consisted of stabbing a child to create an outlet for the spirit to get out of the child. (page 22)

- If child marriage prevalence trends continue, by 2020, 142 million girls will be married before they are adults. (page 24)

- In 2012, 7,885 children and teenagers vanished from care in England and Wales, with at least 2,959 going missing more than once. (page 28)

- 83% of people overall say they are 'concerned' about child pornography with 74% saying they are 'very concerned'. (page 29)

- 0.5-1.5 billion children experience violence each year. (page 32)

- The Children Act 1989 for England and Wales gave children the right to be protected from abuse and defined key elements of the child protection system. (page 35)

- The Sexual Offences Act 2003 was introduced to update legislation relating to offences against children. It includes the offences of grooming, abuse of position of trust, trafficking and covers offences committed by UK citizens whilst abroad. (page 35)

- In the UK, reporting child abuse is currently discretionary. The Republic of Ireland is the only country in the UK in which reporting is mandatory. (page 37)

Child abuse

The emotional, physical or sexual mistreatment of a child.

Child marriage

Where children, often before they have reached puberty, are given to be married – often to a person many years older.

Child Protection Plan

A plan detailing what must be done to promote a child's development and health along with protecting them from further harm.

Emotional abuse

Behaviour which causes emotional damage.

Grooming

Actions deliberately taken by an adult to befriend a child before sexually exploiting or abusing them.

'In need'

If the quality of a child's health or development is likely to be impaired unless provided by a local authority.

Internet Watch Foundation

A charity that works to minimise the availability of child abuse images and other criminal adult content on the Internet.

Faith-based abuse

Child abuse or other crimes that can be linked to faith, religion or belief.

Legislation

A law or body of laws that aim to regulate behaviours or actions.

Mandatory reporting

The reporting of a crime or criminal behaviour that is required by law.

Neglect (emotional and physical)

A failure to sufficiently care for the needs of something or someone.

Physical abuse

An act intended to cause someone else physical harm, pain, injury or suffering.

Sarah's Law

Campaigned for after the murder of Sarah Payne, the scheme allows parents to enquire about a named individual to establish whether they are a known sex-offender. Also called the Child Sex Offender Disclosure Scheme.

Sexual abuse

Causing another person to be subject to undesired sexual behaviour.

Assignments

1. Using the information from this book, write a short paragraph summarising the definition of 'child abuse'.

2. In pairs, discuss the issue of 'neglect'. Write down some examples of neglectful behaviour and then consider the effects that each behaviour might have on a child. For example, failing to keep a child clean and clothed is considered neglectful behaviour and could affect that child's health and experiences at school. Share your ideas with the rest of your class.

3. Create a poster that demonstrates the most important statistics from the graph on page four and the article *Facts and figures about abuse* on page five.

4. What were the key findings of the NSPCC's *How safe are our children?* report. Write a bullet point list of the most important highlights from the extract on pages 7-9.

5. Read the article *Speaking to your children about 'Stranger Danger'* on page nine. In pairs, script a conversation in which a mother or father tries to explain 'Stranger Danger' to their son or daughter. You should consider how old you think the child should be in this situation and think carefully about how you could explain that people who are not strangers can also be dangerous.

6. Social media sites like Facebook make it very easy for people to pretend to be someone they are not. Although there are age-restrictions on Facebook accounts, many children under 12 still manage to create profiles. Create a presentation aimed at 10- to 12-year-olds that explains Internet-based 'Stranger Danger'. Think carefully about how you can highlight the risks in a way that is engaging and age-appropriate.

7. Read *Shock toll of child-on-child abuse* on page 13. In small groups discuss why you think so many cases of abuse by under-18s are occurring. Do you think that access to pornography and the Internet are influencing young peoples' behaviour? Debate your ideas and then summarise your discussion for the rest of your class.

8. Imagine that you volunteer for a charity such as ChildLine. You receive a call from a 12-year-old boy who is worried that his friend is being neglected. He says that his friend regularly arrives at school in dirty clothes and is always hungry. What would you advise your caller to do? Discuss your answer in pairs or small groups.

9. What is faith based abuse? Create an information leaflet that will be distributed at your school and in your local community. The leaflet should raise awareness of the issue but take care not to encourage prejudice or discrimination.

10. Imagine you work for a charity which campaigns against child marriage in the UK. Write a blog-post for your charity's website explaining the issues surrounding child marriage and your feelings about the issue. Read the article *A childhood lost* on pages 24-25 for information.

11. Write an article for your school/college newspaper explaining why it is important to seek help if you have been sexually abused. Include some information about charities and centres that can help.

12. Imagine that you are the head master/mistress of a secondary school in the UK. You are concerned about the issue of child sexual exploitation and decide to write a letter that will be sent home to parents, warning them of the issue. Create a draft of this letter, explaining child sexual exploitation and the warning signs. You should also include advise on where parents can go for help and support if they are worried about their son/daughter.

13. Choose a point on the history of child protection timeline on page 35 and research it further. Write a short article discussing your findings.

14. Read the articles *UK 'should follow Ireland by making it mandatory to report child abuse'* on page 37 and *Charities call for 'mandatory reporting' in the UK* on page 38. In pairs, create a campaign to raise awareness of the petition from the NAPAC. You could choose a TV campaign, a radio campaign, posters on the London Underground network or a combination of all three.

Acknowledgements

While every care has been taken to trace and acknowledge copyright, the publisher tenders its apology for any accidental infringement or where copyright has proved untraceable.

Illustrations:

Pages 2 & 34: Don Hatcher; pages 13 & 16: Simon Kneebone; pages 6 & 22: Angelo Madrid.

Images:

All images are sourced from iStock, Morguefile or SXC, except where specifically acknowledged otherwise.

Page 21 © Tim Bouwer

Additional acknowledgements:

Editorial on behalf of Independence Educational Publishers by Cara Acred.

With thanks to the Independence team: Mary Chapman, Sandra Dennis, Christina Hughes, Jackie Staines and Jan Sunderland.

Cara Acred

Cambridge

September 2013